Rhinegold Re

Edexcel A2 Music
Revision Guide

by

Alistair Wightman

R·

Rhinegold Education
239–241 Shaftesbury Avenue
London WC2H 8TF
Telephone: 020 7333 1720

10.95

Music Study Guides

GCSE, AS and A2 Music Study Guides (AQA, Edexcel and OCR)
GCSE, AS and A2 Music Listening Tests (AQA, Edexcel and OCR)
GCSE Music Study Guide (WJEC)
GCSE Music Listening Tests (WJEC)
AS/A2 Music Technology Study Guide (Edexcel)
AS/A2 Music Technology Listening Tests (Edexcel)
Revision Guides for GCSE (AQA, Edexcel and OCR), AS and A2 Music (Edexcel)

Also available from Rhinegold Education

Key Stage 3 Listening Tests: Book 1 and Book 2
AS and A2 Music Harmony Workbooks
GCSE and AS Music Composition Workbooks
GCSE and AS Music Literacy Workbooks
Romanticism in Focus, Baroque Music in Focus, Film Music in Focus, Modernism in Focus,
The Immaculate Collection in Focus, Who's Next in Focus, Batman in Focus, Goldfinger in Focus,
Musicals in Focus
Music Technology from Scratch

Rhinegold also publishes Choir & Organ, Classical Music, Classroom Music, Early Music Today, International Piano,
Music Teacher, Muso, Opera Now, Piano, The Singer, Teaching Drama, British and International Music Yearbook,
British Performing Arts Yearbook, British Music Education Yearbook, World Conservatoires,
Rhinegold Dictionary of Music in Sound

Other Rhinegold Study Guides

Rhinegold publishes resources for candidates studying Drama and Theatre Studies.

First published 2010 in Great Britain by
Rhinegold Education
239–241 Shaftesbury Avenue
London WC2H 8TF
Telephone: 020 7333 1720
Fax: 020 7333 1765
www.rhinegold.co.uk

© Rhinegold Publishing Ltd 2010

You should always check the current requirements of the examination, since these may change.
Copies of the Edexcel specification may be downloaded from the Edexcel website at www.edexcel.com
Telephone 01623 467467 Fax 01623 450481 Email publications@linneydirect.com

Edexcel A2 Music Revision Guide
British Library Cataloguing in Publication Data.
A catalogue record for this book is available from the British Library.
ISBN: 978-1-907447-03-7
Printed in Great Britain by Headley Brothers Ltd

Contents

THE AUTHOR

Alistair Wightman read Music at Oxford and then York University, where he was awarded a D.Phil for his study of the music of Karol Szymanowski. He has worked in primary, secondary and further education, and is tutor in Aural Training at the Stafford Music Centre. He is also a freelance teacher and writer, and serves as a principal examiner in history and analysis in A-level music with one of the English awarding bodies. In addition to appearing as a pianist, both as a soloist and as a member of the Chiarina Trio, he continues to pursue his interests in Polish music, his publications including several books and articles devoted to Tadeusz Baird, Karlowicz and Szymanowski.

ACKNOWLEDGEMENTS

The author would like to thank the consultant Hugh Benham and the Rhinegold editorial and design team of Adrian Horsewood, Harriet Power, Katherine Smith and Richard Gumbley.

Introduction

For the Edexcel A2 qualification in music you have to complete the following parts:

◆ Unit 4 – Extended Performance (30% of the total A2 mark)
◆ Unit 5 – Composition and Technical Study (30% of the total A2 mark)
◆ Unit 6 – Further Musical Understanding (40% of the total A2 mark).

This revision guide will help you revise for Unit 6, an externally assessed examination which lasts two hours. The paper is divided into three sections, and this guide deals particularly with Sections B (Music in context) and C (Continuity and change in instrumental music). Section A (Aural analysis) is thoroughly covered in Rhinegold's *Edexcel A2 Listening Tests*.

The mark total for Unit 6 is 90, distributed as follows:

◆ Section A: 28
◆ Section B: 26
◆ Section C: 36

At the start of the summer term, it is quite likely that you will still have to finish Units 4 and 5. Try to complete these assignments as promptly as possible in order to make more time to revise for the Unit 6 examination.

SET WORKS

The set works change annually, so make sure you study the correct music for the year you are taking the examination. All the prescribed works are taken from the *Edexcel A-level Music Anthology* (EMA) edited by Julia Winterson (Edexcel, 2008), and details are given below. Bear in mind that, though based on music which may well be unfamiliar to you, Section A (Aural analysis) questions will focus on genres or styles that you have studied for Sections B and C. Note that the specification (syllabus) requires you to study two areas of study: Applied Music and Instrumental Music.

Applied Music 2010

◆ EMA 7:   Stravinsky – *Pulcinella* Suite: Sinfonia, Gavotta and Vivo
◆ EMA 14:   Gabrieli – Sonata pian' e forte
◆ EMA 36:   Purcell – 'Thy hand, Belinda' and 'When I am laid in earth' from *Dido and Aeneas*
◆ EMA 44:   Goldsmith – *Planet of the Apes*: The Hunt (opening)
◆ EMA 59:   Gong Kebyar de Sabatu (Bali) – *Baris Melampahan*

Instrumental Music 2010

◆ EMA 6:   Tippett – Concerto for Double String Orchestra: movement I
◆ EMA 10:   Cage – Sonatas and Interludes for Prepared Piano: Sonatas I–III
◆ EMA 15:   Corelli – Trio Sonata in D, Op. 3 No. 2: movement IV

- EMA 16:   Haydn – String Quartet in E♭, Op. 33 No. 2 ('The Joke'): movement IV
- EMA 17:   Beethoven – Septet in E♭, Op. 20: movement I
- EMA 23:   Schumann – *Kinderscenen*, Op. 15: Nos. 1, 3 and 11
- EMA 48:   Louis Armstrong and his Hot Five – *West End Blues*

Applied Music 2011

- EMA 28:   J. S. Bach – Cantata No. 48, 'Ich elender Mensch': movements I–IV
- EMA 40:   Schoenberg – 'Der kranke Mond' from *Pierrot Lunaire*
- EMA 43:   Bernstein – *On the Waterfront*: Symphonic Suite (opening)
- EMA 45:   Williams – *ET*: Flying Theme
- EMA 61:   Niall Keegan (Ireland) – *Tom McElvogue's* (jig) and *New Irish Barndance* (reel)

Instrumental Music 2011

- EMA 2:   Haydn – Symphony No. 26 in D minor, 'Lamentatione': movement I
- EMA 13:   Holborne – Pavane 'The image of melancholy' and Galliard 'Ecce quam bonum'
- EMA 18:   Brahms – Piano Quintet in F minor, Op. 34: movement III
- EMA 21:   J. S. Bach – Partita No. 4 in D, BWV 828: Sarabande and Gigue
- EMA 25:   Shostakovich – Prelude and Fugue in A, Op. 87 No. 7
- EMA 49:   Duke Ellington and his Orchestra – *Black and Tan Fantasy*
- EMA 50:   Miles Davis Quintet – *Four* (opening)

Both areas of study for each year must be tackled, as Section B (Music in context) draws on the Applied Music list, and Section C (Continuity and change) on Instrumental Music works.

SECTION A (AURAL ANALYSIS)

There are two questions in the examination:

- Comparison of two excerpts of music by the same composer
- A general test of aural perception, involving notation of a melody (both pitch and rhythm), commenting on specific compositional devices (keys, chords and cadences) and providing information on the historical context.

You should practise as frequently and as regularly as you can, making sure you form the habit of:

- Seeing how many marks are available (and therefore how much information is required)
- Working out plausible possibilities (e.g. related keys) to support your impressions
- Using correct terms (keep referring to the glossary at the end of this guide).

In the comparison question, be prepared to answer questions on:

- Instruments and/or voices
- Textures
- Rhythmic devices and patterns
- Melodic aspects
- Features of word-setting
- Keys, cadences and chords
- Harmonic devices
- Historical context (genre, composer, date).

> Useful resources are the Sample Assessment Materials (Edexcel, 2007, publications code UA018895) and *Edexcel A2 Listening Tests* (Rhinegold, 2010).

Remember that in examinations you find yourself in an artificial situation. You are often tested on the various skills you learn separately, but in spite of this try not to let your own approach become rigidly compartmentalised. Try to appreciate musical works as a whole, and apply the knowledge you gain in one area of your activities to other aspects of your musical investigations: for example, your study of harmony should also help your listening and exploration of musical styles.

SECTIONS B AND C

The rest of this book is aimed at helping you to:

- Organise the information you have already collected (and may still be collecting)
- Focus on the demands of questions which are set in this exam
- Improve the way you express your ideas.

You may take an unmarked copy of the Anthology into the exam, and this in itself is a valuable aid to you if you can find your way round the scores quickly and efficiently. It will help if you keep listening to your prescribed works so that you begin to recognise and locate the key features we shall be looking at. Obviously, it makes much more sense to be able to locate features you require in the score itself than to try to memorise whole chunks of information.

Demands of Sections B and C

In Section B, you answer two out of three options, all dealing with music in context. In other words, the questions will involve showing how features of musical style relate to the historical background or the purpose of the work. The works are all taken from the Applied Music list, and by definition have some sort of function (e.g. incidental music, music for opera or some sort of ceremony).

In Section B, you may answer in note form if you prefer, without the risk of incurring any penalty. Each option is worth 13 marks, giving a total of 26 for the section. Do not waste time answering the third option as well – you won't gain any more marks, and may well jeopardise your chances of producing a well-written essay in Section C.

In Section C, you must answer one question of the two set on Instrumental Music. You should write in continuous prose, as your essay will be assessed both for the information it contains and the way you have expressed yourself.

The total mark for the essay is 36, and we shall see how marks are allocated in the samples which follow.

In Edexcel's Sample Assessment Materials you will see holistic descriptors for each question set in both sections B and C. The examiners will, naturally, take into account the number of correct, relevant and valid points made by the candidate. They will also evaluate the quality of the writing (Quality of Written Communication – QWC), and this will involve such aspects as:

> The holistic descriptors are a hierarchy of words – from 'Outstanding' to 'Poor' – each with a range of marks and a brief description of the attributes of an answer at that level.

◆ Organisation, planning and coherence

◆ Syntax and spelling

◆ Use of appropriate terminology.

We have seen already that in Section B you may answer in note form if you wish. You will, however, have to be careful to express yourself as clearly as possible, arranging your ideas together into a logical, coherent sequence.

We have provided examples of mark schemes (indicative content) and specimen answers with commentaries for you to study. Some answers have been left unmarked for you to evaluate. We have also suggested short exercises aimed at helping you to improve the way you present your ideas. Naturally, you will be most interested in the set works for your year, but find time to glance at the remaining specimen answers as suggestions are made throughout the guide on how to improve your quality of written communication.

One of the most common reasons for losing marks is irrelevance. Always stick to the point, and always take care to write about the works specified in the question.

Do not worry if, sometimes, you seem to be stating the obvious! And always take care to pile up examples. Many candidates fail to earn high marks because they neglect to pursue the line of enquiry as thoroughly as possible. For example, if the question concerns tonality, then you should try to give as much detail as possible about how the composer modulates, right the way through the piece.

Think about how best to organise your time when answering questions. You do not have to worry about Section A, as the CD organises timings for you. For the rest of the paper, for which you will probably have approximately an hour and a half, you could experiment with taking about 20 minutes for each of the Section B options, and about 50 minutes for Section C. Try to allow some time for reading through your work before handing in your answer book.

Useful additional reading

➤ *Rhinegold Dictionary of Music in Sound* by David Bowman (Rhinegold, 2002)

➤ *Writing about Music Workbook* by Alistair Wightman (Rhinegold, 2008)

➤ *Edexcel A2 Music Study Guide* by David Bowman and Paul Terry (Rhinegold, 2009).

SECTION B: Music in Context (Applied Music) 2010

Set out below are examples of the types of question normally set in this section of the paper. Read them through carefully so that you are sure about the sort of information you are required to provide. If you are uncertain about what is meant, refer to the glossary at the end of this book.

SAMPLE QUESTION (A)

Describe features of Gabrieli's Sonata pian' e forte which are typical of Venetian Renaissance music. (13)

Mark scheme

Before studying the mark scheme (indicative content) which follows, attempt the question yourself. Notice that the key words are 'Venetian' and 'Renaissance', so you should think about the circumstances of performance as well as the more general Renaissance features of the work. The question is open-ended: in other words, it does not specify particular features to be described. In such cases, try to comment on rhythm, melody, harmony, tonality, texture, performing forces and genre or structure.

Indicative content	
Points should be illustrated with examples from the music.	
Rhythm	Limited variety of note lengths
	Final part of piece uses shorter note-lengths
Melody	Relatively restricted range
	Frequently conjunct, the largest interval being an octave with 4ths and 5ths occurring more frequently
Harmony	Root-position and first-inversion chords predominate, with the occasional consonant 4th
	Cadences include perfect, imperfect (Phrygian) and plagal Tierces de Picardie
	Various suspensions
Tonality	Dorian mode on G
	Cadences on various degrees of mode producing 'wandering' tonality
Texture	Polychoral
	Antiphonal
	Mainly contrapuntal, with some occasional homophony
Instrumentation	Uses typical Renaissance instruments – cornett, old violin (with a range similar to the modern viola) and trombones (or sackbuts).
	Writing is not yet idiomatic, the music showing signs of vocal styles
Structure	Through-composed, revealing links with sacred vocal works (e.g. motet)

Context	Designed for performance in St. Mark's Cathedral, Venice, thus allowing use of spatially separated galleries, in this case involving two four-part groups.

The expression 'indicative content', used by examination boards, simply refers to the sort of information that examiners look for when marking students' exam papers.

Because you take an unmarked copy of the anthology into the exam room, your music examples should normally be bar and part references where appropriate. You will gain no further credit for copying out passages of music, and merely lose valuable time.

Sample answer 1

Gabrieli's work stands on the borderline of Renaissance and Baroque music. Some works, such as the motet *In ecclesiis*, show definite signs of the Baroque (with the use of continuo instruments and the combination of voices and instruments). In contrast, Sonata pian' e forte is quite old-fashioned and in many ways shows stylistic traits of the Renaissance era.

> A good opening paragraph, establishing the historical context.

This is immediately apparent in the instrumental writing. Although he specified particular instruments, such as violin, cornett and trombones, his writing for them is not idiomatic, and in fact looks more as though it derives from vocal models [1], especially the sacred music of the 16th century. This in itself has an influence on the nature of the melodic writing. Stepwise writing is frequent [1], and leaps are rarely more than a 4th or 5th [1]. Harmony and tonality also contain aspects which point towards the Renaissance. The work is modal, being written in the Dorian mode on G [1]. Gabrieli cadences on most steps of the Dorian scale, leading to a fluid tonal scheme [1], e.g. G at bar 25, C at bar 31, B♭ at bar 43 and D at bar 54. Cadences include perfect (e.g. bar 25), Phrygian (bars 16–17) and plagal at the end [1]. As often happens in music of this period, tierce de Picardie [1] is frequently used at ends of sections, and also at the close of the work. Texture is also typically Renaissance. Often the music is contrapuntal [1], and from bar 71, there is a series of close imitations [1] in most of the eight parts, contributing to much of the excitement in the closing stages of the work.

> Good use of examples.

	The characteristically Venetian aspects of the music
	come with the division of the eight parts into two groups
	of four instruments. These would have been placed in
	separate galleries in St. Mark's Cathedral, Venice [1],
	where Gabrieli was organist and director of music.
	It allows him scope for striking antiphonal exchanges [1]
	and grandiose tuttis.
	Overall, the work is highly typical, both of Venetian
	methods of the times and older Renaissance music
	in general.

Examiner's points

This was a very good answer with 11 observations and six clearly located supporting examples or groups of examples. It was coherent and well-expressed, and would have been awarded full marks. Notice that not all observations can usefully be supported by examples, such as the general point that the work is in the Dorian mode in G. There is indeed little point in giving examples of features which occur throughout, such as stepwise movement.

Exercise

List further features which the candidate could have included.

Sample answer 2

- Written for solemn occasion – could have been Mass or a Saint's Day – St Peter's Rome. Coro I in one gallery, Coro II in another [1].

  > Not enough for a mark.

- Stereo effects.

  > An unhelpful remark. The candidate would need to comment further.

- Dynamics. Softs and louds.

  > The observation has been accepted, although antiphony would be a more suitable term when writing about older music.

- Uses instruments, but writing seems more suited to voices [1].

- Call-and-response used frequently [1].

  > Again the observation has been accepted, although the remark is a sweeping generalisation.

- Very scalic [1].

- False relations, e.g. bar 30 with A and Ab.

  > In fact, there are no false relations in this work. It seems the candidate has misread the tenor clefs.

- Lots of suspensions [1]. See cornett in bars 1–2 [X].

  > Tied notes do not always indicate the presence of a suspension.

- Grand finish with all parts playing a big perfect cadence [X].

- Tierces de Picardie at ends of phrases [1], see bar 17, C♯ [X].

  > A tierce de Picardie only occurs when the tonic minor chord becomes major. In this instance the phrase finishes on the dominant of D minor with a Phrygian cadence.

Examiner's points

This sort of response just comes into the 'adequate' category. There are six valid observations, but no satisfactory illustrations. The note-form response is not here presented in a logical manner, and the sweeping nature of some points and poor grasp of terminology also weaken the general impression.

The overall mark would be 6/13.

Exercise

Remove the incorrect or unhelpful observations, and rewrite in complete sentences. Provide examples where appropriate.

Sample answer 3

Mark this answer yourself, commenting at the end on its good points, but also mentioning ways in which it could have been improved. Check your assessment against the examiner's points which follow after completing your marking.

	Sonata pian' e forte shows many features of Renaissance music. It is modal as it is in Dorian mode, transposed to G, and the harmony is characterised by almost constant use of Picardy thirds, e.g. at the end.
	Textures are clearly Renaissance style, being mainly contrapuntal. Much of this counterpoint is free, with the parts independent of each other, but Gabrieli also uses some imitation, particularly near the end.
	Rhythms are typical of this period as they are rather simple, though again at bar 71 things become more complicated, and there is even some syncopation (in the cornett).
	An important feature of Sonata pian' e forte is the use of antiphony. This often occurs in Venetian music as the building the music was meant to be played in – St Mark's – has widely-spaced galleries for musicians. This was ideal for playing off different groups against each other.

Examiner's points

The credit-worthy points are as follows:

- Modal, Dorian in G
- Tierce de Picardie with example
- Contrapuntal
- Imitation (but the location was insufficiently precise for credit)
- Basic rhythms
- Syncopation at bar 71
- Antiphony
- St Mark's galleries.

The total was eight points, not all illustrated when possible. Such a response is regarded as competent. The writing was coherent, though it would have been possible to deal with textural features (counterpoint and antiphony) together. Clearly, very much more could have been included.

Exercise

List additional points which the candidate could have made. Provide a final 'summarising' sentence to round off the answer.

SAMPLE QUESTION (B)

How does Goldsmith convey primitivism in his music for *Planet of the Apes*: 'The Hunt'? (13)

Mark scheme

Before studying the mark scheme (indicative content) which follows, attempt the question yourself. Notice that the key word is 'primitivism'. This question is also open-ended, so try to comment on such aspects as rhythm and metre, melody, harmony, tonality, texture, and performance forces.

Indicative content	
Points should be illustrated with examples from the music.	
Rhythm and metre	Time signature changes
	Driving rhythms involving ostinati
	Heavy accentuation, e.g. opening bars
Melody	Angular
	Chromatic
	Serial manipulations
	Recurring motifs
Harmony	Dissonant
	Chords derived from tone-row
Tonality	Non-functional
	Tonal references by way of pedals
Texture	Homophony at opening
	Polyrhythms at various points
Instrumentation	Symphony orchestra with large percussion section
	Ram's horn, Tibetan horn intensify primitive atmosphere
	Electronic instruments
	Extremes of instrumental ranges
	Loud dynamics.

Sample answer 1

Cut to close up: heads of frightened primitives	
Orchestration	
• Large orchestra ◄————————————	Not enough detail for a mark.
• Special diagetic effects, e.g. ramshorn, producing primitive hunting calls [1].	
Harmony	
• Mainly dissonant [1]	
Melody	
• Jerky broken-up lines hopping around [1 – accept], but some long notes as well ◄———————	Not enough detail.
Rhythm	
• Driving riffs [1]	
Metre	Confused statement which overall gives a misleading impression.
• Stays pretty constant [X]	
• Atonal throughout, except when there are pedals ◄——	
• Prominent piano part ◄—————	Unhelpful remark.
• Violins play 'naturale' – another way of saying primitive [X].	
• Lots of rushing scales ◄————	Not enough.
• Closes suddenly without proper conclusion – doesn't even have a double bar, showing just how crude it is. ◄——	Another unhelpful interpretation.

Examiner's points 🖋

There were four unillustrated points. At best this response would be regarded as 'basic'. There was no proper organisation, and there were numerous misunderstandings. This answer would receive 4/13.

Exercise

Rewrite the correct observations in complete sentences, and supply examples to illustrate the points made.

Sample answer 2

Planet of the Apes was a film version of a French novel written in 1963, using science fiction to investigate man's superiority and arrogance by showing these failings by way of a world in which apes control enslaved humans. The violent images and strange background to the film are reflected in the modernistic style of Goldsmith's score, which ranges from minimalist single-note effects (in the opening titles) to maximal effects, reserved for dramatic scenes such as 'The Hunt', which consists of a full five-minutes continuous playing-time in the complete film version.

> Although a little background or context may be helpful, this opening paragraph is over-extended. Remember, you are probably limiting yourself to about 20 minutes for this question, so it is better to focus immediately on the demands of the question.

Goldsmith conveys the alien, primitive aspect of the scene by making the score as little like traditional, 'civilised' music as possible. Unlike the folk-music origins of Titanic or the tonal big tune of E.T., Goldsmith produces a score which is serialist [1], a technique associated with the 2nd Viennese School (Schoenberg, Berg and Webern), who produced notoriously difficult music. Fittingly for a sci-fi piece, the musical technique is highly modernistic as it involves the use of a 12-tone row, announced in bars 8–9 [1], which is presented in different forms, e.g. inversion, when the ideas are upside down, retrograde when they go backwards, and retrograde-inversion, when they do both.

> This is a purely abstract description of some of the techniques applied by Goldsmith, and at best would gain perhaps one further mark.

> At last!

> Good example.

The note-row can also be used to form chords [1], and because the composer has to use the notes in the order they come in the row, he cannot normally produce consonant harmonies. This can be seen in the opening, highly dissonant [1] bar of the score, which involves three chords: notes 1–4 of the row form chord 1, notes 5–8 chord 2 and 9–12 the last chord of the bar [1]. Another really dissonant moment occurs at bar 42, when all 12 notes are heard coming in in reverse order [1].

> Illustration of point.

Another obviously primitive feature of the score is the instrumentation. Goldsmith uses a lot of percussion, e.g. timpani at the start, and later boo-bams, timbales, friction drum, vibra slap and conga drum [1]. In addition he uses Ram's horn and Tibetan horn [1] which are very fitting, given that the music is meant to be a hunt.

> More examples.

	Goldsmith also produces primitive effects by making
	the instruments play at the extreme ends of their ranges
	[1], e.g. horns at the top end, as well as piccolos and
	flutes doing the same.
	This score clearly shows how well Goldsmith
	understood the effect music can have in enhancing
	visual images.

Examiner's points

Nine points, with limited illustration. The main problem arose from the writer's reluctance to tackle the specific demands of the question. It was however coherent and well-expressed, and would be regarded as 'confident' work, gaining 9–10/13.

Sample answer 3

Mark this answer yourself, commenting at the end on its good points, but also mentioning ways in which it could have been improved. Check your assessment against the examiner's points which follow after completing your marking.

	Planet of the Apes is fundamentally about primitive
	situations involving violence. One of the most famous
	scenes is the Hunt, and here Goldsmith provided
	a score which underlined graphically the fear of the
	hunted and the aggression of the hunters. To do this,
	he used primitive devices, but also a highly modernistic,
	technically sophisticated musical style.
	The primitive aspects are immediately evident in the
	selection of instruments. As part of a massive orchestra,
	Goldsmith incorporates boo-bams, ram's horn and also
	electronic instrumental effects, e.g. the clarinet squeaks.
	For much of the time, the dynamic is loud producing a
	fiercesome effect. Even when the volume drops, Goldsmith
	keeps the tension at fever pitch by way of urgent rhythms,
	seen in the driving ostinati, e.g. at b. 11 which periodically
	returns in different keys as the excerpt progresses.
	At other points, Goldsmith introduces repetitive
	figurations, e.g. bar 84 in woodwinds, combined with
	another ostinato and also a cross-rhythmic effect where
	groups of three quaver lengths (dotted crotchets) are
	heard against the prevailing four crotchet pulse. Perhaps
	there is a hint of African drumming effects here.

	Repeated rhythmic patterns occur from the very
	start, e.g. the opening triple-time pattern repeated three
	times. This, with the highly percussive first beat (piano
	and timps) gains much of its force from the dissonance.
	This in turn comes from Goldsmith's use of serialist
	techniques. It is clear enough that the work is partly 12-
	tone, as a 12-note row appears in full melodically in bars
	8–9, being hinted at in bar 4. Bars 1–3 however, consist
	of chords put together from the notes of this row, with
	notes 1–4 in chord 1, 5–8 in chord 2 and 9–12 in chord 3.
	Later all twelve notes are heard together at bar 42.
	All these features contribute to the primitivism of
	the scene.

Examiner's points

This was a very good response, with 13 points receiving credit:

* Ram's horn
* Electronic effects
* Loud dynamics
* Urgent rhythms (with example)
* Repetitive figuration (with example)
* Combination of ostinati (with example)
* Cross-rhythm (with example)
* Highly percussive first beat
* Dissonance (with example)
* Serialism
* Note-row with location
* Chords in bar 1
* All 12 notes together (illustrated).

The writing was coherent, and the candidate would receive full marks.

Exercise

List other points which the candidate could have made.

SAMPLE QUESTION (C) ❓

Identify features of 'Thy hand, Belinda' and 'When I am laid in earth' from Purcell's *Dido and Aeneas* (EMA 36) which are characteristic of English Baroque music. (13)

Mark scheme ✏

Before studying the mark scheme (indicative content) which follows, attempt the question yourself. Notice that the key words are 'English' and 'Baroque'. This question is also open-ended, so try to comment on such aspects as rhythm and metre, melody, harmony, tonality, texture, structure and performance forces. You may find it convenient to start with the broad historical context.

> For more information on Baroque music see Hugh Benham, *Baroque Music in Focus* (Rhinegold, 2007).

Indicative content	
Points should be illustrated with examples from the music.	
Structure/genre	Opera Subject drawn from classical antiquity Recitative and Aria Recitative prepares for Aria's single emotional state Aria uses ground bass Five-bar ground Concluding ritornelle
Rhythm	Speech rhythm predominates in recitative Triple time in Aria Hemiola at cadences Scotch snap
Melody	Chromatic inflections Some leaps, including falling diminished and perfect 5ths Vocal melody's phrasing often at odds with ground bass Varying phrase lengths Anticipations and cadences
Harmony	Suspensions Final chord an open 5th
Tonality	'Free' fluctuating scheme of recitative characteristic of early and middle Baroque Aria anchored to G minor by ground bass
Texture/forces	Continuo Small string orchestra Melody and broadly homophonic accompaniment.

Sample answer 1

Purcell was a mid-Baroque English composer whose
work reveals French and Italian influences in spite of its
markedly English feel. *Dido and Aeneas* was his only true
opera [1], though a number of other stage works, such as
Fairy Queen, *King Arthur* and *Indian Queen*, also show his
skills with staged music.

> Good context.

> Further useful context.

The extract in the anthology consists of a recitative
and aria [1], also commonly encountered in Italian music
from the mid-seventeenth century onwards. The external
trappings are also typically Baroque with basso continuo
(harpsichord or lute) supporting the solo voice in the
recitative with improvised chords [1]. In this work, the
supporting band is restricted to strings [1] as was
frequently the case in this period. A further indication
of foreign influence is the fact that the concluding
instrumental passage is labelled ritornelle [1], while
the ground bass [1], a typically Purcellian method, was
popular with Italian composers such as Monteverdi
and Cavalli. The unusual thing about this ground bass
is that it is five bars in length [1], its shape marked by
a chromatic descent [1]. Not only that, the vocal line's
phrases rarely coincide with the bass, e.g. the opening
phrase which begins on the last chord [1], and at bar 21, a
vocal phrase is heard running over the end of one playing
of the bass and start of the next [1].

> Good examples.

Also typical of the age and genre is the subject
matter which is taken from ancient sources [1]. These
had been popular from the very beginnings of the Baroque,
e.g. Monteverdi's *L'Orfeo* and *Il ritorno d'Ulisse*.

The division of recitative and aria is also very
characteristic, with speech rhythm especially prominent
in the recitative [1]. Purcell also introduced striking
speech rhythm effects in the course of the aria, e.g.
'Remember me'. Harmony is also typical, with use of
suspensions [1].

Examiner's points

12 points, some illustrated. This work would gain full marks. It was well-written and also provided historical background. It could have ended more elegantly, and perhaps the candidate could have focused a little more on purely technical matters.

Exercise

Provide detailed examples of suspensions (remember these can be 4–3, 7–6, 9–8 and 2–3, where these figures indicate the interval above the bass).

Sample answer 2

• Written for a girls' school in Chelsea	Irrelevant here.
• Based on classical content, like Blow's *Venus and Adonis* [1]	
• Blow was organist at Westminster Abbey	
• Purcell was also organist there	
• He wrote a lot of church music, and music for the stage, but Dido was his only opera [1 – accept]	
• This is the dramatic final scene, when Dido kills herself, probably with a dagger in the final section	
• First section is a recitative with speech rhythm [1]	
• There is no speech rhythm in the Aria, which is more song-like	Not strictly true.
• It is in regular time	Unhelpful.
• Uses a harpsichord, which shows it is Baroque [1]	
• Authentic performances should use a harpsichord or perhaps a lute. The string players should also use authentic instruments, and especially the proper type of bow. They should not use vibrato.	Well-meant advice, but irrelevant here.
• Purcell uses a ground bass [1]	
• Unusually it lasts 6 bars	Miscounted bar numbers.
• Very dissonant.	True, but suspension must be mentioned to gain the mark here.

Examiner's points

Five points, with no useful illustration. The writing showed no real organisation, with little connection made between points. This work was barely adequate, and would gain 6/13.

Exercise

Retain the correct observations, and add three more relevant points, providing illustrations wherever appropriate.

Sample answer 3

Mark this answer yourself, commenting at the end on its good points, but also mentioning ways in which it could have been improved. Check your assessment against the examiner's points which follow after completing your marking.

Purcell's *Dido and Aeneas* was composed in 1689 and so is clearly middle-Baroque and is also a good example of the English approach to Baroque music.

It is an opera, which is in itself a Baroque invention, and this excerpt consists of a recitative and aria, reflecting the move to divide the opera into passages which told the story or established the dramatic situation – the recitative – and more lyrical sections – the arias – which allowed the characters to reflect on the situation. Generally the recitatives used more speech-like rhythms for clarity, and so there was often syllabic word-setting, though here Purcell uses some melisma to allow some key words, such as 'darkness', to be emphasised.

Another Baroque invention was the continuo, here taken by a harpsichord (or lute), which provided supporting harmonies. The other accompanying instruments were strings, just a small band of them, typical of the middle Baroque period.

A final characteristic device of the period was the ground bass. It was used from the earliest years of the Baroque by Monteverdi among others, and was one of Purcell's favourite devices. Here he shows his ingenuity by writing a five-bar ground, which is often out of step with the vocal line with regard to phrasing, e.g. the vocal phrase at bars 19–22 which goes over the end of one playing of the bass at bar 21, and the start of another.

The work provides a useful demonstration of Baroque harmony. There are many suspensions, e.g. a 4–3 at the start of the concluding passage for strings alone, a double 7–6/4–3 in the next bar, while the characteristic anticipation effect is found at the end of the vocal solo in bar 45. The vocal part in the recitative also contains a 9–8 suspension at the start of bar 4.

There are many other aspects of this work which are typical of both Purcell, and the Baroque in general, but I've run out of time.

Examiner's points 🖊

The candidate made 11 points altogether, some of them well-illustrated:

- ◆ Opera
- ◆ Recitative and Aria
- ◆ Speech rhythm
- ◆ Some melisma
- ◆ Harpsichord continuo
- ◆ Small string band
- ◆ Ground bass
- ◆ Five bars long
- ◆ Overlapping of vocal phrases and ground bass, with illustration
- ◆ Suspensions and the illustrations
- ◆ Anticipation.

> Be sure you understand fully the harmonic devices mentioned in this section. It will also help you in Unit 5. For further information, see Hugh Benham, *A2 Music Harmony Workbook* (Rhinegold, 2009).

It was well-written, though the apologetic final paragraph was unnecessary. This work would have been awarded full marks, even though further relevant points could have been made.

Exercise

List additional points the candidate could have made, and provide appropriate illustrative examples.

SAMPLE QUESTION (D)   ❓

Diaghilev asked Stravinsky for arrangements of various 18th-century works for the ballet score of *Pulcinella*. Focusing on harmony and texture in 'Gavotta con due variazioni', offer reasons for Diaghilev's initial shocked reaction to the result. (13)

Before studying the mark scheme (indicative content) which follows, attempt the question yourself. Notice that the key words are 'harmony', 'texture', 'Gavotta con due variazioni' and 'shocked reaction'. You may find it convenient to refer briefly to the historical context, but take care to keep your remarks relevant. Do not waste time on any aspect of the 'Gavotta' which is not to do with harmony and texture.

Indicative content

Points should be illustrated with examples from the music.

Harmony	Functional framework (derived from the model) with perfect cadences
	Original modified by addition of pedals, and horn appoggiaturas
	Other noteworthy features:
	43–44: tonic chord clashes with subdominant chord
	51: random (unprepared) dissonance in oboe 2 line
	69: modulation to A major weakened by ambiguous G♮ in bassoon
	76: unprepared dissonance in flute
	79: oboe 1 has new counter-melody creating suspensions
	80/83: weakened cadences
Texture	Scored for wind instruments only
	Instrumentation aimed at producing typical Neoclassical objective/non-expressive/anti-Romantic sound
	The original basic two-part texture expanded by addition of countermelodies (e.g. horn in bar 39)
	Additional accompaniment figuration
	Sustained notes
	Glissandi in bassoon
	Alberti bass in bassoon
	'Tirade' effects (rapid runs) in the two flutes.

The horn parts here are particularly wide-ranging. Notice that they are notated in both treble and bass clefs as needed. Remember that if in the treble clef, horn in F sounds a 5th lower than notated, while in the bass it sounds a 4th higher.

Sample answer 1

Harmony in the 'Gavotta' is basically traditional, as is the form which is binary. The first section, up to the repeat sign at bar 10, starts in D and as expected moves to A major, and the second section modulates more widely. There is a section in G to begin with, then a sequential repeat in A, then a series of cadences in F♯ minor, E minor and D, where the music closes eight bars later. The variations as might be expected, all follow the same pattern.

There is much good detail, but, alas, it is all irrelevant. 'Traditional' harmony is not precise enough at this level to gain credit, and, strictly speaking, modulation and changes of key will come under the heading of tonality.

Cadences also follow traditional 'functional' patterns [1] with e.g. imperfect cadence at bars 4 and 10 [X].	One of the striking aspects about the harmony of the 'Gavotta' is that all the cadences are perfect.
There are also many examples of 'wrong-note' harmony which was typical of the Neoclassical style developed in the 1920s [1]. There is a glaring clash at the beginning of the 'Gavotta', where the horn C♯ is heard against the D in the oboe [X].	The candidate has forgotten that the horn is a transposing instrument.
Textures are also quite different from the original by Monza which was mainly in two parts. Stravinsky scored this movement for woodwinds and brass, seeking to avoid the over-emotional sonorities of the string section [1 – accept]. Because he included many more instruments, the textures are obviously thicker, and they become even more thick when Stravinsky adds extra lines, especially obvious in Variation 1 at bar 50 where the second oboe is given a new part [1].	Try to avoid 'thick' and 'thin' as descriptions of textures at this level.
In many ways, Stravinsky retains original aspects of the Monza with trills and the like, though he does sometimes make the melody jerkier than it was in the 18th-century version.	Good example.

Examiner's points

The candidate made four partly illustrated points. It was well-written, but marred by irrelevance. Harmony should primarily concern chord structure, chord progressions (including cadences) and dissonance treatment. The answer would gain 5/13.

Exercise

Help the candidate to raise the mark by suggesting a further two harmonic and two textural points, with appropriate examples.

Sample answer 2

Diaghilev expected a straightforward transcription for orchestra, as Tommasini had done with Scarlatti sonatas for Les Femmes de bonne Humeur. Stravinsky kept the basic structure and content of the originals, in this case the theme and two of the six variations from a suite by Monza, but added touches which brought the work right into the 1920s.

	Harmonic effects include:
	• Pedals which blur the harmony, e.g. the tonic pedal which sounds through chord V of the perfect cadence in bars 27–28 [1]
	• Clash of a full G major chord and D major chord in bars 42–43 [1]
	• Modulation to A major at bar 69 made ambiguous by G♮ rather than G♯ [1].
	Textural effects include:
	• Additional 'tirade' effects in the flutes at bar 73 [1]
	• Alberti bass in bassoons, e.g. bar 65 [1]
	• Glissando effects, also in bassoon at bar 15 [1].
	There are therefore many additional 'shocking' elements to the score.

> Notice that the mark is awarded here not for the modulation to A, but the weakening of the perfect cadence.

Examiner's points

The candidate made six fully illustrated points. Notice the successful combination of a continuous-prose general introduction and bullet-point listing of technical features. This work would be deemed competent, and gain 8/13.

Exercise

Expand upon the remark about the 1920s at the end of the opening paragraph.

Sample answer 3

Mark this answer yourself, commenting at the end on its good points, but also mentioning ways in which it could have been improved. Check your assessment against the examiner's points which follow after completing your marking.

	Stravinsky's score is the first of his Neoclassical works, and the start of what proved to be the longest creative phase of his career, lasting over 30 years and culminating with *The Rake's Progress* in 1951.
	There were already hints of the style in the preceding years, e.g. *The Soldier's Tale*, so it could be said that Diaghilev should have realised what he was in for.
	The basis for *Pulcinella* was a series of pieces by Gallo, Pergolesi and Monza, among others, but instead of simply arranging them, Stravinsky 're-composed' them, as he put it.
	'Gavotta and two variations' was based on a keyboard work by Monza, and its basic two-part texture

was expanded for the woodwind and brass sections of the band. Stravinsky had already used this sort of group in his Symphonies for Wind Instruments, and many other works of the 1920s make more use of these parts of the orchestra at the expense of the strings (e.g. Piano Concerto and Symphony of Psalms) as part of an anti-Romantic reaction.

The expansion of the original to involve several instruments meant additional melody lines and doublings. Some of these additions include the Alberti bass in Variation 2, the rapid runs in the flute and the additional melody lines, e.g. the horn figures in the main theme at bar 11 and the additional oboe lines at bar 51, for example.

Stravinsky also introduced some unusual timbres, notably the glissando effects in the bassoon and the rather high horn parts.

Many of the textural additions have some bearing on the harmony. Inevitably, this is basically traditional with cadential progressions, all of which are perfect. But the cadences are frequently undermined, e.g. right at the close which fizzles out with an open octave, while in the first-time bar, the dominant chord is not followed by a full tonic chord, but a thinly textured return to the Alberti figuration.

Other ways that Stravinsky peps up the harmony involve the adding of pedals, e.g. at 26–28, where the inverted tonic pedal sounds right through the perfect cadence, including the dominant chord. Elsewhere he allows a complete clash of D and G chords (bar 44). Additional lines, such as the oboe in bar 51, introduce random unprepared dissonances which sound mildly shocking.

Diaghilev may have been shocked by what Stravinsky did to the 18th-century material, but the result is a charming introduction to a particular type of 20th-century style, perfectly matching the mischievous onstage action.

Examiner's points

This well-written account provided good historical context, and incidentally linked the additional textural elements to the harmonic style. The credit-worthy points were:

* Woodwind and brass instrumentation
* Anti-Romantic reaction
* Alberti bass

- Rapid flute runs
- Additional horn and oboe lines
- Bassoon glissandi
- High horn parts
- Perfect cadences
- Undermining of cadences
- Pedals
- Superimposed D and G chords
- Unprepared dissonance.

There were 13 appropriately illustrated points, thus gaining full marks.

Exercise

Collect information on the harmony and texture in the remaining movements and make notes also on melody, rhythm, structure and tonality for the complete work.

SAMPLE QUESTION (E)

Identify rhythmic and melodic features of *Baris Melampahan* that indicate that it is an example of gamelan music. (13)

Before studying the mark scheme (indicative content) which follows, attempt the question yourself. Notice that the key words are 'rhythm', 'melody' and 'gamelan'. You may find it convenient to refer briefly to the work's context, but take care to keep your remarks relevant. Do not waste time on any aspect of *Baris Melampahan* which is not to do with rhythm and melody.

Indicative content		
Points should be illustrated with examples from the music.		
Rhythm		Regular pulse throughout
		Until the slowing down at the close of the extract
		Constant 'on-beat' pulse with some 'off-beat' sounds from the gangsa, sangsih and polos
		Kendhang rhythms are occasionally displaced
		Organised in rhythmic cycles, gongans
		Consisting of 4 keteg
		Each keteg lasting 4 (or 8) beats
		Gongs mark end of each cycle

Melody	Based on a 'nuclear' melody
	Involving pitch numbers 1, 2, 3, 5 and 6 from the *pelog* scale
	Known as the *pelog selisir*
	Difficult to describe component intervals because of tuning which differs from e.g. European tuning
	Frequent repetitions
	Heard in varying degrees of completion
	The only significant departure occurs at [H], the 'High Tune'

Sample answer 1

Baris Melampahan is part of a much longer piece of music designed to portray a dramatic scene of a warlike nature. The dance here is in modern Balinese style, and is typified by sudden outbursts, e.g. the loud angsel, vivid contrasts occurring when the melody transfers to a higher pitch [1] and most of all its dazzling, shimmering percussion sounds.

The piece is built round a nuclear melody [1], the main theme, which is played on the balungan instruments. This basic melody is constantly repeated [1], and is based on notes 1, 2, 3, 5 and 6 of the pelog scale [1], a seven-note scale. This set of notes is known as the pelog selisir [1], which is a little different from the more frequently encountered slendro, a five-note set.

Rhythm is controlled by the gongan [1], a rhythmic cycle composed of four four-beat groups [1], termed ketegs [1], and percussion instruments provide a strong pulse throughout [1], with gongs marking the end of each cycle [1].

One of the very characteristic elements of gamelan music is the use of a beating effect called the ombak, caused when pairs of metallophones are tuned lightly out of tune with each other, so giving the music its typical sound quality.

This paragraph is really concerned with timbre and so is not relevant.

The other characteristic feature is the use of heterophony, arising from the way the panusan instruments decorate the nuclear melody.

A textural point, and therefore irrelevant.

Examiner's points

The candidate here made 10 points, but there was also some irrelevance. The work would gain 11/13.

> ### Exercise
> Add two more points, providing illustrative examples.

Sample Answer 2

	Rhythm
	• Gongs mark divisions between the cycles [1]
	• The cycles are called gongans [1]
	• They consist of 4 ketegs [1]
	• Ombak effects.
	Melody
	• Nuclear melody [1]
	• Treated heterophonically
	• Alternates with angsel and Kendhang [1]
	• Based on 5 pitches – selisir pelog [1].

Examiner's points

The candidate made six basic points in a rather sketchy way. At most, it would gain 7/13.

> ### Exercise
> Rewrite the candidate's statements in continuous prose to remove ambiguity.

Sample answer 3

Mark this answer yourself, commenting at the end on its good points, but also mentioning ways in which it could have been improved. Check your assessment against the examiner's points which follow after completing your marking.

	The war-like qualities of this piece, played by a group
	based right in the central region of Bali, are conveyed by
	the insistent rhythms, maintained until the very close
	of the extract where there is a slowing down. The music
	has a distinct four-beat feel, and each rhythmic cycle
	(gongan) consists of four four-beat bars or ketegs.
	The overall impression is quite different from Western

> music as the instruments are tuned differently. In fact tuning varies from region to region, and the impression is further complicated by the fact that the metallophones are often slightly out of tune with each other, producing the ombak effect.
>
> Gamelan music is based on the pelog scale. This consists of seven notes, but in this case the music draws on only five pitches (C#, D, E, G#, A) as given in the preface in EMA, though these pitches are only very approximate. At some points, the music moves into a higher pitch region (the high tune), but the group sticks to the same basic pitches, an octave higher.
>
> The tune is initially heard on the ugal, the largest of the two-octave metallophones, and later is heard decorated on the gangsa, sangsih and polos, producing the heterophonic effect which is so characteristic of gamelan music. The basic four-bar phrase is often repeated, producing the characteristic hypnotic effect of this music.
>
> This is communal music, and the whole village takes part in the performance.

Examiner's points

Credit was awarded for mention of:

* Insistent rhythms
* Slowing down at end of piece
* Gongans
* Ketegs
* Four four-beat cycles
* Tuning
* Five-note scale
* Higher pitches
* Repetition.

Nine points with little illustration. It was well written, but marred by some irrelevance.

It would gain 10/13.

Exercise

Draw up revision notes for this piece on texture, timbre, structure and circumstances of performance.

SECTION C: Continuity and Change in Instrumental Music 2010

Set out below are examples of the types of question normally set in this section of the paper. Read them through carefully so that you are sure about the sort of information you are required to provide. If you are uncertain about what is meant, refer to the glossary at the end of this book.

SAMPLE QUESTION (A)

Michael Tippett Concerto for Double String Orchestra: movement I (EMA 6)
Beethoven Septet in E♭ Major, Op. 20: movement I (EMA 17)
West End Blues **(EMA 48) as recorded by Louis Armstrong and his Hot Five**

Compare and contrast the approach to rhythm in the three pieces listed above. (36)

Before studying the mark scheme (indicative content) which follows, attempt the question yourself. Notice that the key word is 'rhythm'. You may find it convenient to refer briefly to the context of each work, but take care to keep your remarks relevant. Do not waste time on any aspect of the listed works which do not concern rhythm and the related topic of metre.

Indicative content	
Points should be illustrated with examples from the music.	
Tippett	$\frac{8}{8}$ time signature, permitting irregular subdivisions, i.e. 3+3+2, and 2+3+3 at the end
	Occasional deviations to $\frac{6}{8}$ and $\frac{4}{8}$
	Syncopations
	Generally constant flow of quavers
	Conflicting 3+3+2 and half-bar lengths (e.g. quaver, crotchet, quaver)
	Rhythm augmented at bar 95, and doubled again at bar 99
	At bar 118, longer values in lower parts heard against shorter values in upper parts

Beethoven	Slow triple-time introduction followed by quick duple-time movement
	Slow section uses full range of note values from whole bar lengths to demisemiquavers
	Sextuplets
	Triplets
	Constantly moving quavers in inner parts of Allegro
	Bass part at first consists of one note a bar on first beat
	Anacrusis of three quavers
	Syncopations in inner parts in some sections
	Diminution in closing bars
Armstrong	Free-rhythm introduction with pause
	Triplets
	Dotted rhythms
	Head has crotchet anacrusis made up of dotted-note figure
	Some dotted rhythms are notated as Scotch snaps
	Comping accompaniment consists of steady crotchet chords
	Trombone solo typified by longer notes
	Scat singing involves triplet and sextuplet semiquavers
	Piano solo contains demisemiquavers
	The most sustained/lengthiest notes of piece occur in final chorus.

Sample answer 1

The Beethoven is the earliest of the three works to be considered, and I shall deal with that first as the rhythmic style is quite different from Tippett's and Armstrong's.

The Beethoven Septet opens with a slow introduction in triple time [1], and embraces a wide range of note values, some lasting a whole bar (dotted minim), others only demisemiquavers [1]. Beethoven also uses sextuplets at e.g. bar 14 in the wind section and bars 17–18 in the strings [1].

The main part of the work is in fast duple time, and there is nothing here which departs from classical styles. The main theme opens with a three-quaver anacrusis [1] and is accompanied by an inner part of uninterrupted quavers [1] and a bass part of single notes appearing on main beats only [1] until near the end of the first statement, where Beethoven doubles the pace to increase the tension (bar 27). This typically is linked to the increasing harmonic pace of the music near the cadence [1]. Other rhythmic features of this movement are triplets at bar 76 [1] and the rhythmic diminutions, again linked to increased harmonic pace, in the final bars [1].

Good observation.

Tippett's Concerto for Double String Orchestra and West End Blues, featuring Louis Armstrong, though very different in style, are both 20th-century works, separated by only a few years. It is arguable that Tippett's music shows the influence of jazz, as well as the early English madrigal, Stravinsky and Beethoven (though not in the rhythms). The concerto has an unusual time signature of 8 quavers a bar [1] which allows for subdivisions of bars into irregular groupings. Most typical of these is 3+3+2, most evident in bar 15 [1] where the conductor is supposed to give three beats in the bar. Occasionally Tippett reverses this pattern to 2+3+3, as in the final stages of the piece [1]. Apart from this the piece is syncopated [1] almost the whole time, and Tippett also uses conflicting rhythmic groups simultaneously, e.g. the two half-bar groupings with syncopation heard against the 3+3+2 groupings at bar 80 [1]. As opposed to Beethoven, Tippett uses rhythmic augmentation, first at bar 95 where the previous quaver patterns become crotchets [1], and again at bar 99 where the pattern is changed to minim lengths [1].

Additional example accepted.

West End Blues is typically relaxed in its rhythmic writing, obvious from the very start of the rubato style introductory bars [1], with triplets [1], a pause which weakens the sense of pulse still further [1] and dotted rhythms [1]. The simple quadruple pulse [1] is established at the start of the main part of the piece where there are steady crotchet accompanying chords. As the piece goes on, time values become shorter, most obviously in the florid demisemiquaver flourishes.

Examiner's points

There were 26 appropriately illustrated points. The work was well-organised and well-written, and it was a good idea to deal with the chronologically earliest work first, in spite of the order given in the question. In fact, there was no reason why

West End Blues should not have been discussed before the Tippett, especially in view of the candidate's valid observation on some of the influences on Tippett's work. It was a pity there was no conclusion, and for this reason an examiner would probably give a mark in the region of 32/36 (i.e. at the lower end of the top, 'outstanding' band).

Exercise

Write a concluding paragraph, attempting to show which work, in your opinion, reveals the most original approach to rhythm.

Sample answer 2

Tippett	Beethoven	West End Blues
$\frac{8}{8}$	$\frac{3}{4}$	¢
Fast	Slow-fast	A tempo
Sonata form	Sonata form	12-bar blues and choruses
Strings	Mixed	Mixed
Mainly counterpoint	Homophonic	Homophonic
Modal	Functional	Substitution chords
Dissonant	Consonant	Consonant
Syncopation [1]	Syncopation [1]	Syncopation [1]
No dotted rhythm	No dotted rhythm	Dotted rhythms [1]
No triplets	Triplets [1]	Triplets [1]
No sextuplets	Sextuplets [1]	No sextuplets

Annotations (right margin):
- It is not enough to copy out time signatures and hope to gain credit.
- Not enough specific information here for a mark
- Irrelevant.
- Irrelevant.
- Irrelevant.
- Irrelevant.
- Irrelevant.
- Marks are not awarded for negative statements.
- Incorrect.

Examiner's points

The candidate here made seven basic points with no illustration. There was considerable irrelevance, and the layout was wrong, i.e. in note form as opposed to continuous prose. In view of this, the work would be assessed as 'limited', and be awarded a mark of 10/36.

Exercise

Rewrite the few correct observations there are in continuous prose, and give examples. Clarify the opening points about time signatures and tempi in such a way as to earn marks.

Sample answer 3

Mark this answer yourself, commenting at the end on its good points, but also mentioning ways in which it could have been improved. Check your assessment against the examiner's points which follow after completing your marking.

Tippett's *Concerto for Double String Orchestra* has a disagreeably frantic feel because of the energetic rhythms. There is constant quaver movement throughout most of the piece, except for a passage in the middle where the note-lengths get longer. The mysterious atmosphere at this point of the movement is emphasised by the augmented triads which destroy any sense of key.

One of the reasons for the very busy feel of this piece is the way Tippett sets one orchestra off against another. Even though the textures are rather thin, the counterpoint means there is something going on the whole time. This obviously affects the rhythm of the piece with different rhythmic groups played off against each other. Tippett uses an unusual time signature of 8 quavers a bar, but these are divided into irregular groups, e.g. 3+3+2 quavers, and it gets really chaotic when he uses it against syncopated quaver-crotchet-quaver groups.

Like Beethoven, Tippett uses sonata form and this helps him keep things under control to some extent. Unlike Tippett though, Beethoven has a slow introduction. This has three beats a bar, and it leads on to the fast section with four beats a bar. This is very regular and to be frank, there is little to discuss about Beethoven's use of rhythm. It's all nice and ordinary, unlike the Tippett, so I'll go on to *West End Blues*.

West End Blues also has a slow introduction, but there is much more variation than in Beethoven's. It has a pause in the middle which stops the pulse. This fits in with the vague tonality which is all over the place. This is not surprising as Armstrong probably made it up as he went along.

> The 12-bar blues itself is much more organised. It is
> in E♭ throughout, and has a steady crotchet beat as well
> in the piano. This is essential, as the top parts are doing
> their own thing with triplets and constantly changing
> patterns. In fact the rhythms are random all the way
> through and if it weren't for the piano keeping time, it
> would not make sense. To help keep the pulse, Armstrong
> says 'Add a milk bottle sound' at one point. They had to
> do this for percussion effects because microphones in
> the 1920s couldn't cope with proper percussion. The piano
> solo is the most interesting section, with its stride bass,
> substitute chords and streams of demisemiquavers.
>   I am going to complain to the Exam Board for setting
> this rubbish question. How on earth am I supposed to find
> 18 things to say about rhythm?

Examiner's points

The candidate made nine points, some illustrated:

* Constant quaver movement
* Rhythmic groups played off against each other
* Irregular groupings
* Syncopation
* Slow introduction with three beats to the bar
* Pause in the middle of *West End Blues* introduction
* Steady crotchet pulse
* Triplets
* Demisemiquavers in piano solo.

Marks would not be awarded for 'energetic rhythms' and 'note lengths get longer' as these remarks were insufficiently precise. The Allegro of the Beethoven is in duple time, not quadruple. Examiners will forgive displays of bad temper, even when unjustified, but not the extensive irrelevance. This work is in the 'adequate' category, and would gain a mark in the region of 18/36.

Exercise

Help the candidate to find a few more things to say about rhythm.

SAMPLE QUESTION (B)

Corelli Trio Sonata in D, Op. 3 No. 2: movement IV (EMA15)
Haydn String Quartet in E♭, Op. 33 No. 2: movement IV (EMA 16)
West End Blues **(NAM 48) as recorded by Louis Armstrong and his Hot Five**

Compare and contrast the approach to structure and tonality in the three pieces listed above. (36)

Before studying the mark scheme (indicative content) which follows, attempt the question yourself. Notice that the key words are 'structure' (i.e. form) and 'tonality' (i.e. keys and modulation). You may find it convenient to refer briefly to the context of each work, but take care to keep your remarks relevant. Do not waste time on any aspect of the listed works which do not concern structure and tonality.

Indicative content		
Points should be illustrated with examples from the music.		
Corelli		Binary form with repeated sections
		Monothematic
		Main theme treated imitatively (fugally)
		In inversion
		In stretto
		Functional tonality
		With cadences
		Pedal points
		And modulation to closely related keys
		First section closes in dominant
		Second section cadences in relative minor, E minor and G major
Haydn		Rondo form
		Functional tonality
		With cadences
		Pedals
		But very few modulations
		E.g. A♭ from bar 36
		F minor from bar 48
		Humorous 'mistreatment' of second-inversion chords at cadences
Armstrong		Twelve-bar head with choruses/variations
		Free introduction touching on C minor, B♭ minor
		12-bar sections in E♭ throughout
		Modified plagal cadence at close.

Sample answer 1

The structures of these pieces are all radically different and to some extent reflect the historical periods in which they were composed. The Corelli is in binary form [1], with the first section from bars 1–19 repeated [1], as is the rest of the piece. It is based on much the same material throughout [1], so the opening idea is immediately imitated in fugal style by the second violin [1], and is later heard inverted at bar 20 [1], where it is also heard in stretto, the second violin coming in after only one bar as opposed to two [1].

> Accept as a non-technical way of saying monothematic.

In contrast, the Haydn movement is in rondo form [1], which means its main theme keeps coming back, separated by episodic material. The main theme, heard in bars 1–8, returns at bar 28, then at bars 71, 99 and 141 [1 further mark].

West End Blues is a 12-bar blues [1], with a six-bar introduction [1], then the Head, which forms the basis for variations [1] for trombone, clarinet and scat voice, piano and finally the complete group. The 12-bar cycle is kept going right the way through the piece without change.

> A somewhat misleading statement as the final version is slightly extended. In other variations, there are harmonic changes which mask the basic harmonic progression.

In some ways, these pieces have more in common with regard to tonality as they all use functional harmony and cadences [1] to define the key, though the odd thing is that the earliest piece is the one which modulates the most [1]. The first section opens in D and at the double bar moves to the dominant, A major [1] with a perfect cadence [1]. In the second part of the piece, Corelli cadences in B minor at bars 27–28 [1], emphasised by the hemiola, a very characteristic device of the period. It then goes on to touch on a variety of other keys before closing in D.

> True, but irrelevant.

> There is not enough detail for a mark here.

Haydn, as already stated, does not modulate as much. Most of the time he stays in E♭ [1], emphasised by constantly repeated cadences, especially at the end [1] as part of the 'joke', and long dominant pedals [1]. In marked contrast, however, he introduces unstable keys at bar 36 where he goes to A♭ [1], but does not resolve the cadential second inversion in the conventional way [1].

The least stable part of West End Blues is the introduction which hints at C minor before the pause [1]. In contrast, the main part of the piece does not move from E♭ at all [1].

Examiner's points

The candidate made 22 points altogether, some of which were well illustrated. The layout was perhaps a little clumsy, and little is gained by considering structure and tonality separately as structure is often defined by handling of keys. There were one of two irrelevant or misleading statements, but overall this essay would come into the 'excellent' category and gain 31/36.

Sample answer 2

Corelli's Sonata is in binary form [1] and has an interesting tonal scheme with the high violins and low bass producing a polarised texture, so producing some striking tone colours, further enhanced by the twang of the harpsichord. Both parts are repeated here [1]. This is in marked contrast to West End Blues where there are no repetitions at all. It goes straight through without stopping, but is divided into sections which clearly have different tone colours. It is more interesting than the Haydn and the Corelli which are only for strings. Armstrong uses trumpet, clarinet and trombone, as well as piano and bass. He even introduces a milk-bottle rhythm (boca-di-boc) and most unusually he uses scat. This is the wordless singing effect, heard here in call-and-response to the clarinet. There are lots of interesting sound effects as a result to keep the listener's interest.

Haydn did what he could with the instruments he had at his disposal. The piece is in rondo form [1], with frequent returns of the main theme. He could have done more to vary this theme, but at least at the end he split it up into a series of short phrases which make it difficult to tell when it finished.

West End Blues is a 12-bar blues [1].

> The candidate has misunderstood tonality.

Examiner's points

There are four points here, with no illustration of devices. The question has been misunderstood in significant measure, and there is no sign of effective planning. It would come in the 'limited' category, and be awarded 10/36.

Sample answer 3

Mark this answer yourself, commenting at the end on its good points, but also mentioning ways in which it could have been improved. Check your assessment against the examiner's points which follow after completing your marking.

Corelli was a mid-Baroque composer, and it is possible to see in his work the workings of the recently invented tonal system, using major-minor keys as opposed to varieties of modal scales. He was an Italian composer who specialised in the writing of concerti grossi as well as trio sonatas, and liked to put on concerts involving large numbers of string players. In spite of this, it is best to perform his work with one player a line, in this case two violins, a bass and the harpsichord to play the harmonies.

Corelli's approach to tonality depends on functional cadential progressions and modulation to related keys. In fact, movement through the keys helps to underline the structure. Like many Baroque composers, he often wrote in binary form (see Bach's suites and partitas), and this is no exception. The key scheme, as stated above, is linked to the structure. The first part ends at bar 19 with a modulation to A major, the dominant. As was customary, in the second part of the movement (from bar 20 to the end), Corelli went through more keys, touching on B minor, the relative minor by bar 28, and then G major at bar 31 and D major at bar 35. Notice also the interrupted cadence at bar 41 before the final phrase brings us home in the last bar.

Haydn also modulates extensively, moving to the dominant Ab at bar 17. Later he touches on F minor (bar 48) before returning to the tonic. He frequently uses pedals, both tonic and dominant, e.g. the tonic pedal on Eb at bar 36. This movement is in rondo form.

The key of *West End Blues* is also Eb, and unlike the earlier pieces, Armstrong keeps in this key throughout. It is a 12-bar blues which means it has a fixed harmonic progression based on chords I, IV and V, varied by occasional substitution chords which can result in circles of fifths. It hints at different keys in the introduction, notably C minor and Bb minor at bar 4 (with the Gb and Db). Another interesting effect comes at the end with the added sixth chord, preceded by a decorated plagal cadence.

Examiner's points

The credit-worthy points are as follows:

* Major-minor tonal system (i.e. functional)
* Cadential progressions
* Modulation to related keys
* Binary form
* A major, dominant
* B minor at bar 28
* F minor at bar 48
* Pedals
* Rondo
* Accept Armstrong staying in E♭ throughout
* 12-bar blues
* Different keys in introduction
* Decorated plagal cadence.

Notice that marks were not awarded for the incorrect key analysis, descriptions of pedals in the Haydn and the circle of 5ths in Armstrong.

Though well-written in general, there was an over-extended introduction which was tending to irrelevance, and the candidate failed to round the essay off. The work would count as competent, and be awarded 23/36.

Exercise

Prune the introduction and provide a conclusion.

SAMPLE QUESTION (C)

Cage Sonatas and Interludes for Prepared Piano: Sonatas I–III (EMA 10)
Beethoven Septet in E♭ Major, Op. 20: movement I (EMA 17)
Schumann Kinderscenen Nos 1, 3 and 11 (EMA 23)

Compare and contrast the approach to texture in the three pieces listed above. (36)

Before studying the mark scheme (indicative content) which follows, attempt the question yourself. Notice that the key word is 'texture'. You may find it convenient to refer briefly to the context of each work, but take care to keep your remarks relevant. Do not waste time on any aspect of the listed works which does not concern texture.

Indicative content
Points should be illustrated with examples from the music.

Cage	Textures include:
	Homophonic
	Monophonic
	Two-part homorhythmic
	Layered
	Texture closely linked to timbre of prepared piano
	Some 'dead' sounds
	Gamelan qualities
Beethoven	Chords for varying numbers of parts
	Monophony
	Antiphonal exchange/dialogue
	Melody-dominated homophony
	Some broken chord accompaniment
	Some syncopated inner parts
	Octaves
	Thematic combination
Schumann	No 1: Mainly in three parts
	Melody + accompaniment with broken chords in middle
	Detached quavers in bass masked by pedal
	3rds in RH at bar 9 in counterpoint with bass
	No 3: Leaping/stride LH with mainly single-line melody
	More sustained writing from bar 13 leading to longer chord at bar 15
	With ascending scale in middle part
	No 11: Three-part, broadening to four parts
	Bass melody with off-beat RH chords
	Chords for all parts.

Sample answer 1

The works are dealt with in chronological order.

    Beethoven disliked the Septet, apparently, because it seemed to him to be too Classical. It is an outstanding example of this style, being fundamentally homophonic in texture [1]. Having said that, he obtained considerable variety within the work, partly by varying the number of players performing at any one time, and also by changing the type of texture used. ◄

1	Tutti chords [1]
2	Monophonic violin [1]
8	Chords in three parts for strings [1]
19	Three-part strings melody-dominated homophony [1] with broken-chord figure in viola
29	Tutti mdh, with syncopated inner parts [1] ◄
40	Monophonic solo violin ◄
47	Antiphonal exchange between wind instruments, answered by strings [1]
86	Three-part string chords ◄
111	Mainly octaves [1] ◄

Schumann only had a piano for this piece, so the range of textures won't be so large.

No. 1: 3-part mdh, with broken chord in middle part [1]

No 3: Oom-pah LH [1] ◄

No 11: Mdh, but here LH has tune sometimes (bar 9) [1]

Cage was also writing for a single piano, but had a much wider range of sounds and timbres because of the preparation [1] which changed the effect, e.g. the occasional clunks and twangs. Some of the basic types of texture are as follows:

Sonata 1: chordal [1], pretty well throughout, but see last line for basic chords.

Cluster chords at bar 10 [1]

Sonata II: single line at start [1] building up to 3 layers at bar 30, with longest notes in bass [1]

Sonata III: Closest to mdh at bar 19, with melody in RH [1] ◄

None of these pieces has much in the way of counterpoint.

Avoid underlinings in continuous prose.

Avoid abbreviations in continuous prose writing.

This type of texture has already been credited.

This has already been credited.

Accept.

Accept.

Accept.

Examiner's points ✒

17 points were made, with some illustrated. Unfortunately, the mark will have to be adjusted because of the wrong format and use of underlinings and abbreviations, none of which should appear in a passage of continuous prose. A mark of 22/36 is appropriate.

Exercise

Rewrite the paragraph on Schumann in continuous prose, expanding on the points already made.

Sample answer 2

Of the three works, the most modern is the Cage, and this is the one with the thickest textures. The preparation of the piano results in a dense, percussive sound. It is sometimes compared to a one-man percussion band and certainly sounds rather like a gamelan. The effects are obtained by putting bits and pieces between the strings to alter the timbre. The first sonata is typified by its use of chords [1]. The first is a G^7, and so sounds quite dissonant, but not as dissonant as the really thick cluster chords in bar 10 [1]. The last type of chord comes in bars 20 to the end, where both hands are in the treble clef.

There are not so many chords in Sonatas II and III, making this music more contrapuntal [X]. There are also a number of trills and flourishes to hold our interest. Another interesting texture effect comes from the pedals.

The earliest piece is the Beethoven Septet. Because there are seven players here, Beethoven could produce some really thick sounds, especially when the strings players double stopped. At times he has all the players at once (tutti), like the chord at the beginning [1]. This is followed straight away with a single violin playing monotony. It goes on like this throughout. Often there are only three players at one time, e.g. bar 19 where the strings have the main theme. Here there are single bass notes and a sort of Alberti bass in the viola [1].

> Unhelpful expression, best avoided.

> Not enough for a mark.

> This remark is unclear.

> An unfortunate use of an incorrect term!

> The remark has been accepted, although properly speaking the viola plays broken-chord figures as opposed to a true Alberti pattern.

Schumann's pieces are intended for children, so there
is nothing very complicated about them. The first one
has triplets throughout, the second one (No. 3) has a ← Not enough.
jazzy stride bass [1] which helps to give the impression
of children running around, while the scary piece at the
end (No. 11) is very creepy and chromatic. Here Schumann ← Irrelevant.
puts the tune into the bass, while the right hand plays
off-beat chords [1].
The Cage produces the most unusual textures, but the
Beethoven is the most approachable.

Examiner's points

There are six points, some of which are appropriately illustrated. There is also irrelevance and misuse of terminology. There is little evidence of planning. This work comes into the 'basic' category, with a mark of 15/36.

Exercise

Correct the errors, and expand the remarks on the Beethoven Septet.

Sample answer 3

Mark this answer yourself, commenting at the end on its good points, but also mentioning ways in which it could have been improved. Check your assessment against the examiner's points which follow after completing your marking.

The most varied textures are to be found in the
Beethoven. This is scarcely surprising as the other two
pieces are for piano. Admittedly Cage prepared the piano,
inserting all manner of objects into the inside of the
piano, and this increased the range of sounds available
to him. Some obvious textures in the Cage are the chords
in Sonata I and the single-line writing in Sonata II (see
opening). He also uses two parts together with the
same rhythms, and in Sonata III there is use of ostinato
accompanying the melody. With Cage, everything is
subservient to the rhythmic schemes, or fractal patterns.
Unfortunately these are inaudible, and the preparation
makes it difficult to talk about what you can hear.
    Working backwards, the Schumann uses melody-
dominated homophony throughout. In the case of the
first piece, he writes a typically romantic texture, with

the melody in the top part, accompanied by triplet broken chords in the middle and supported by quavers in the bass, sustained by way of the pedal. At one point the top part is doubled in 3rds, and is heard in a sort of counterpoint with the bass.

Hasche-Mann has a stride bass accompaniment, with low bass alternating with a higher chord. The most varied textures come in the final piece Fürchtenmachen, which opens with a melody line in the right hand with a rhythmically independent accompaniment from the left hand. At bar 5, Schumann reverses the roles, with the previous melody placed in the left hand. He carries on with this method at bar 9, but here the melody is accompanied with off-beat right-hand chords. Very briefly, Schumann also uses block chords (bar 24).

Beethoven's Septet opens with a chord for all seven instruments, answered by monophonic violin. The introduction also uses homophony for three instruments, and later on the violin is given a rhythmically independent melody line. The first subject of the sonata form proper is given to three instruments in a melody-dominated homophonic texture. The melody is given to the violin, supported by the viola with broken chords and the cello providing intermittent crotchets. When this theme is repeated at bar 29, the clarinet takes the melody, supported by sustained notes on the other wind instruments and syncopations in the upper strings and a steady crotchet figure in the cello. Another textural device is a form of antiphony or dialogue between the wind and strings at bar 47, and Beethoven also uses most of the instruments in octaves at the start of the development.

Of the three works, Beethoven's is the most interesting. He achieves more contrast than can be found in the other works, partly by varying the number of instruments in play as well as changing the textural layout rapidly.

Examiner's points

Credit was awarded for:

- Preparation of piano
- Chords in Sonata I
- Single line
- Two-part with same rhythm
- Ostinato with melody (allowed, thought the use of the term ostinato is a little dubious)
- Melody-dominated homophony in Schumann
- Implied three parts in No. 1
- Broken-chord middle part
- Bass part
- Upper part in 3rds with bass counterpoint
- Stride bass
- Reversal of left- and right-hand roles
- Off-beat chords
- Block chords
- Tutti chord in Beethoven
- Monophonic line
- Three-part chords
- Description of texture at bar 19
- Description of texture at bar 29
- Antiphonal exchange
- Octaves.

There were 21 valid points, many well illustrated. The essay was well-written and had some sort of plan in that it worked backwards chronologically, keeping the Beethoven to the end. There was a little irrelevance, but this work would be placed in the top category with 32/36.

Exercise

Using your study guides and any other sources you have, draw up revision notes for all the instrumental works for 2010, making sure you are equipped to write on rhythm, metre, melody, harmony, tonality, structure, texture and general context and circumstances of performance.

SECTION B: Music in Context (Applied Music) 2011

Set out below are examples of the types of question normally found in this section of the paper. Read them through carefully so that you are sure about the sort of information you are required to provide. If you are uncertain about what is meant, refer to the glossary at the end of this book.

SAMPLE QUESTION (A)

Bach's Cantata No. 48, 'Ich elender Mensch' (EMA 28) was intended for performance in the course of a Lutheran service in an important German church. What aspects of the work indicate its origins? (13)

Mark scheme

Before studying the mark scheme (indicative content) which follows, attempt the question yourself. Notice that the key words are 'Lutheran', 'important German church' and 'origins', so link the circumstances of performance as far as possible to the compositional features of the work. The question is open-ended, in other words, it does not specify particular features to be described. In this case, try to focus on performing forces and genre to begin with.

The expression 'indicative content', used by examination boards, simply refers to the sort of information that examiners look for when marking students' exam papers.

Because you take an unmarked copy of the anthology into the exam room, your music examples should normally be bar and part references where appropriate. You will gain no further credit for copying out passages of music, and merely lose valuable time.

Indicative content

Points should be illustrated with examples from the music.

Performance forces	Relatively large for a church, indicating wealth, i.e. strings, oboes, trumpets as well as organ continuo, SATB chorus and vocal soloist
	Technical difficulties of both choral and instrumental writing indicate presence of professional musicians
Genre	Cantata, closely linked to the theme of the day
	Major role of chorale (for congregational use)
	German language (as opposed to Latin)
Structure	Multi-movement work
	Besides chorale, use of full range of Baroque styles and techniques:
	• Recitative to make the message clear
	• Aria for reflection on the religious theme
	• Large-scale chorus to set tone, featuring:
	• Ritornello structure
	• Fugal elements
	• Canon on cantus firmus (another chorale melody, used in the final movement of the cantata – not included in EMA).

As previously mentioned, examiners arrive at a final mark for these questions using a holistic grid. (For full details see Edexcel's Sample Assessment Materials, page 93.) For the present, it is enough to know that the full 13 marks will be awarded to work which contains at least nine relevant, well-illustrated points, showing excellent organisation and planning, and expressed coherently without significant spelling or grammatical errors.

As you work through this book, and see examples of work of different standards, you will see how the holistic grid is applied across the available mark range.

Sample answer 1

'Ich elender Mensch' (Unhappy man that I am) is one of the many cantatas Bach wrote during the final period of his career as Kapellmeister of St. Thomas's Church in Leipzig, a major centre in Eastern Germany. This church was Lutheran, and as the question implies, was wealthy and able to hire the best musicians of the day.

The first indication that this was written for an important, wealthy church is the sheer size of the orchestra [1]. It requires trumpet, oboe 1 and 2, soprano, alto, tenor, bass, violin I/II, viola, continuo, and Bach also requires a vocal soloist for the middle movements.

The cantata is also written on a large scale for a piece of church music, compared with e.g. the Bruckner 'Locus iste' and 'The Lamb' by Tavener, both of which consist of just a single movement. In contrast, the Bach consists of four different movements [1], starting with a chorus for all performers, and finishes with an aria [1].

The fact that it is a religious piece is shown by the presence of the chorale, a sort of German hymn, which was meant for the congregation to sing as well as the choir [1]. The text is in German, as opposed to the Latin used in the Roman Catholic churches [1].

> All this is correct, but there is nothing here that would earn marks as yet. Remember you probably have about twenty minutes to answer this type of question, so you need to get on with it!

> It is not necessary to mention every single instrument individually, and it is certainly not a good idea simply to list the instruments and voices as they are laid out in the score without further comment.

> Not enough for a mark.

> The mark is awarded for 'multi-movement' although in fact the cantata actually consists of seven movements.

> More information about the chorus is required for an additional mark.

Examiner's points ✒

The candidate made five observations of a rather general nature, and would probably be awarded 6/13 ('adequate'). There was a lack of focus on the aspects of the work that mattered, and an absence of corroborating detail.

Sample answer 2

- Bach was a Lutheran composer working in Leipzig, where he produced cantatas for each Sunday and Feast day throughout the year.
- The cantatas were usually performed before the sermon, and were linked to the readings of the day.
- Bach had a large group of musicians he could draw on, although in his final years at Leipzig it seems as though resources may have shrunk.
- So the wealth of the church – St. Thomas's – is shown by the size of the performing group (with oboes and trumpets as well as the basic strings and continuo group, four-part chorus and soloist) [1].
- The piece is on a grand scale, with several movements [1], and to be able to produce this sort of work on a weekly basis with limited rehearsal time, Bach must have had a fair number of professional players – also indicating that the church could afford to pay for this type of music [1].
- The Lutheran aspect is immediately clear from the presence of the chorales [1] – hymns often dating back to the Reformation period, or else taken from even older plainsong and fitted with German words [1].
- Chorales designed for congregational use with orchestral doubling to help performance [1].
- Movement I also contains a chorale melody (the same as the chorale used in the seventh movement of the cantata).
- This chorale melody is the cantus firmus [1] which is played in canon [1] by the trumpet and oboe.
- The canon is just one strand in a ritornello movement [1], a complicated form of writing for church music, again showing that Bach's church could afford good performances.

Good context, although there is nothing here so far which would gain a mark.

This and the preceding point could have been combined in a single bullet point.

Point accepted.

Examiner's points

The candidate made nine points, some partially illustrated. There was a degree of repetition, but the most important points were safely made. The work would probably be awarded 10/13 ('confident').

Exercise

Pick out examples of needless repetition, and rewrite these points more economically.

Sample answer 3

Mark this answer yourself, commenting at the end on its good points, but also mentioning ways in which it could have been improved. Check your assessment against the examiner's points which follow after completing your marking.

> The Lutheran cantata was the most important type of music in the German Protestant church. Although the texts, and often the chorale tunes, were adapted from older Catholic sources, they were translated into German so that they were understood by the ordinary church-goer who was also able to take part in the hymns or chorales – such as No. 3 in EMA 28. The texture here is simpler, more chordal, and the parts are doubled by the orchestra so as not to put the congregation off.
>
> The rest of the piece is more complex and shows that the church where Bach worked must have been able to afford lavish performances. This work requires trumpet and oboe as well as strings, although this is still not such a large band as Bach used in the St Matthew Passion with its two orchestras, two choirs and soloists.
>
> The church was still clearly an important patron in Germany, in spite of the Reformation.

Examiner's points

Marks would be awarded here for: use of German language, the presence of a chorale, orchestral doubling in the chorale, its chordal texture and the orchestral forces employed.

Some idea of the work's context was evident, but there were comparatively few observations. It would gain 6/13 ('adequate').

Exercise

Expand on the points made above, and add further observations on the work's structure.

SAMPLE QUESTION (B) ❓

'Disturbed' and 'disoriented' are expressions which have been used to describe Schoenberg's *Pierrot Lunaire*. Describe elements of 'Der kranke Mond' (EMA 40) which support such a view. (13)

Mark scheme ✏

Before studying the mark scheme (indicative content) which follows, attempt the question yourself. Notice that the key words are 'disturbed' and 'disoriented'. This question is also open-ended, so try to comment on such aspects as rhythm and metre, melody, harmony, tonality, texture, and performance forces.

Indicative content	
Points should be illustrated with examples from the music.	
Subject matter	One of a series of poems by Giraud concerning a moonstruck clown
Tonality	Atonal
	Chromatic
Texture	Lean single line accompaniment/absence of harmonic support
Melodic style	Angular
	Irregular phrasing
Rhythm	Irregular patterns make pulse difficult to discern
Techniques	Sprechgesang/pitches not clearly focused
Structure	Through-composed
	Verse refrains ignored in musical setting.

Sample answer 1

Schoenberg, a leading exponent of Expressionism in the years immediately preceding the First World War, remarked of *Pierrot Lunaire* that it was written in an ironic and satirical vein. In fact, with subject-matter based on a clown whose sanity is in doubt [1], it has become an almost classic example of 'disoriented' and 'disturbed'. It is not difficult to see how this has come about. The work is highly chromatic [1] and brings in all 12 pitches of the chromatic scale within the first few bars. It is so chromatic that it is mainly atonal [1].

	Structure is another area where the disturbed nature of the poem is shown. The poem has a refrain, but Schoenberg deliberately avoided using it, and his setting is through-composed [1], without any repetitions at all. The pulse is difficult to make out [1]. There are occasional silences [1], and the melody is full of large awkward leaps [1]. The singer has to use sprechgesang [1], and the off-centre pitches also have a disruptive feel to them. Another destabilising effect comes with the thin accompaniment – just a single flute – and the absence of harmony [1]. Pierrot Lunaire was an epoch-making work that came to be regarded as an archetypal example of this composer and the period in which he worked.

This is misleading, as there is repetition in the vocal line in bars 23–25, the last repetition involving rhythmic augmentation.

Point accepted.

Examiner's points

The candidate made nine relevant points, with limited illustration. This work is basically well-written and shows some sense of the historical context. It would be awarded 9/13 ('confident').

Exercise

The candidate could have improved on the mark by illustrating the points about pulse and an angular melody line. List examples of irregular rhythmic patterns and large intervals.

Sample answer 2

Schoenberg was a pioneering composer whose work was atonal [1]. He invented serialism, which meant the use of 12-note tone-rows, i.e. all 12 pitches used one after another. These rows can then be inverted, retrograded or both together. All 12 notes are used in the first three bars of EMA 40, so showing a serialist approach.

> This is a highly misleading statement. *Pierrot Lunaire* is extremely chromatic, but was composed some years before the development of serialism.

Schoenberg's music is not easy-listening, and this is hardly surprising as the subject matter is about derangement [1]. The whole work is about a clown teetering on the brink of insanity, and if he wasn't feeling disoriented and disturbed to begin with, he certainly was by the time Schoenberg had finished with him! He writes the oddest stuff here. Unlike say the Bach cantata, which has solid harmonies supporting the voices, all Schoenberg uses is a single flute [1]. This must have made it very difficult for the singer to keep in tune, and what makes it even worse are the horribly difficult melody lines with huge leaps [1] and awkward chromatic passages [1], e.g. the serial passage at the start [X].

> In spite of the error regarding serialism, the observation about chromaticism is accepted here.

In the end, it probably does not matter that much if the singer is a bit off-pitch as it can add to the atmosphere, and anyway Schoenberg wants the singer to use sprechgesang [1], a sort of half-speech/half-song effect which frankly makes the singer sound like an amateur who hasn't got her act together.

Examiner's points

There were six general observations here in a piece that was not entirely relevant. It would be awarded 6/13.

Exercise

Rewrite the first paragraph to provide the reader with more reliable historical context.

Sample answer 3

Mark this answer yourself, commenting at the end on its good points, but also mentioning ways in which it could have been improved. Check your assessment against the examiner's points which follow after completing your marking.

	Features contributing to disorientation and disturbance are:
	• Atonality. This produces an intentionally unstable sound. There is no fixed point in the music which allows the listener to feel secure.
	• This suits the subject matter which concerns the 'deathly sick moon of night' with pale blood born of torment.
	• To emphasise the unhinged nature of the text, Schoenberg uses Sprechgesang, a sort of speech-song which often involves notes being voiced in such a way that the pitch is uncertain, i.e. unstable.
	• The vocal writing is intentionally awkward with large leaps, made all the more difficult by the absence of a full harmonic accompaniment.

Examiner's points

The candidate made five clear points: atonality, subject matter, Sprechgesang, large leaps and lack of harmonic support. Unfortunately, the response stopped dead in its tracks after a promising start, and could only be awarded 6/13. It made a pleasant change to see Sprechgesang with an upper case S!

Exercise

Finish off the above response, providing also some supporting references for the point about large leaps. Try to make the last bullet point a summarising, concluding remark.

SAMPLE QUESTION (C)

On the Waterfront (EMA 43) concerns the struggle of an individual against powerful vested interests set in a bleak urban landscape. What aspects of Bernstein's treatment of rhythm and orchestral texture help convey an appropriate mood for the film? (13)

Mark scheme

Before studying the mark scheme (indicative content) which follows, attempt the question yourself. Notice that there are many key words: 'struggle', 'individual', 'bleak' and, of course, 'rhythm' and 'orchestral texture'. You may find it convenient to refer briefly to the dramatic context of the music, but take care to keep your remarks focused on rhythm and orchestral textures.

Indicative content		
Points should be illustrated with examples from the music.		
Rhythm		Bleak landscape underlined by slow opening section (Andante)
		Individualism conveyed by relatively free tempo
		Alternating $\frac{4}{4}$ and $\frac{3}{4}$
		Triplets
		Struggle evident in Presto barbaro with alternating duple- and triple-time bars and tension in main theme
		Main theme characterised by quaver followed by much longer length
		Another recurring pattern consists of two semiquavers and longer note
		Homorhythm at climax underlines violence of struggle
Texture		Andante opens with bleak texture of monophonic horn
		Followed by canon involving flutes and trombone and
		Melody supported by pedal
		Presto: tension of struggle in layered texture ('fugue')
		Riff supporting solo saxophone (representing the individual)
		Then woodwinds and trumpet
		Tutti homophony at bar 78
		106: chords built up note by note
		108: sustained strings as backgrounds to short, hammered chords in remainder of orchestra.

Notice the use of transposing instruments in this score:

Clarinet/bass clarinet in B♭	Sounds a major 2nd below written pitch
Alto saxophone in E♭	Sounds a major 6th below written pitch
Horn in F	Sounds a perfect 5th below written pitch
Trumpet in B♭	Sounds a major 2nd below written pitch

Sample answer 1

As a film score, *On the Waterfront* is perhaps less successful than some as it is almost too sophisticated for the purpose. There are undeniably effective moments in the writing. The idea of the individual against a corrupt society is conveyed at the start by the solo horn melody, which establishes the key centre of F, using the blues scale. The writing is especially high and goes up as far as B♭.

> This comment is not precise enough to gain the mark. An instrument can fulfil a solo role but still be accompanied.

> Irrelevant.

> Candidate has ignored effects of transposition.

The theme is then treated in canon [1] with Tbn 1 following Fl 1, 2 after two beats [1]. The rhythms include triplets [1]. This opening section is slow, and involves changes of time signature.

> Copying abbreviated instrumental names rather than giving the proper full name is insufficient for a mark.

The Presto also uses alternating bars and the harsher sounds here hint at the menacing dockland scene. It opens with a piano and percussion fugue [1]. This is dissonant as the second set of timps come in on C♯, making it difficult to tell what the key is. It stays like this all the way to the end. In fact, Bernstein uses bitonality to hide the key still further near the end.

> Additional detail accepted.

> Not precise enough for a mark.

> Still not precise enough!

One of the most dramatic passages occurs at bar 78 when he has the whole orchestra hammering out the presto rhythm at the same time in dense chordal textures [1], creating a brutal effect. Other interesting effects come earlier with the alto saxophone solo and supporting riff [1], perhaps portraying the individual pitted against his environment.

> Irrelevant.

> Irrelevant.

Examiner's points

The candidate made six relevant points, mainly with illustrations or locations. There were a number of irrelevant comments, but also some occasions where the point was not expressed clearly or fully enough for a mark. This work would receive 7/13 ('competent').

Exercise

Help the candidate score full marks by rewriting some of the woolly statements and by cutting out the irrelevant sections.

Sample answer 2

Rhythm
- Contrasts 'free-style' opening with rigid mechanical style in Presto, symbolising individual pitted against environment [1]
- And slower Andante [1]
- In quadruple time with occasional triple time bars [1]
- Uses triplets (in Andante) [1]
- The lone individual could be represented in Presto with jagged main theme (sax) with quaver followed by longer note lengths [1]
- This idea developed to become two semiquavers and longer note. [1]

Texture
- Thin, bleak sounds
- E.g. monophonic horn, representing the lone hero [1]
- Canon between flutes in octaves and trombone [1]
- Pedal accompaniment to second half of main theme with additional lower part [1]
- Presto opens with percussion and piano motif which is treated as a sort of fugue [1]
- Resulting riff supports alto saxophone melody representing individual [1]
- Melody then scored for woodwind and trumpet [1]
- Tutti homophony ← Location needed.
- Sustained strings and SD ← Not precise enough.
- Staggered build up of chord. ← Location needed.

Examiner's points

12 points made, though not generally well located; the note-form presentation resulted in some slack writing. This work would be considered 'confident' rather than 'excellent', and would be awarded 10/13.

Exercise

Give exact bar-locations for the points made by this candidate.

Sample answer 3

Mark this answer yourself, commenting at the end on its good points, but also mentioning ways in which it could have been improved. Check your assessment against the examiner's points which follow after completing your marking.

On The Waterfront is set in the violent world of the New York docklands during the 1950s, and concerns the struggle of the Marlon Brando character against corrupt union bosses. Bernstein conveys both aspects in the Symphonic Suite derived from the original score.
The horn at the start perhaps stands for the solitary hero. It is heard completely unaccompanied at the start before going into a canon for flute and trombone. This opening is melancholy, and nothing in particular stands out, making it sound bleak.
The Presto is different as it is fast and aggressive with a theme for piano and percussion. Bernstein gradually builds up the texture layer by layer, with the first layer in a sort of G minor and the second layer in C♯. A third layer is provided by the three tuned drums. Put together, this gives a riff which goes on for some time under the sax melody. This is repeated for the whole wind and brass section. The climax comes at bar 78 with the whole orchestra playing the rhythm of the riff in chords.
Rhythms in this section are more complex with alternating time signatures and choppier rhythms.

Examiner's points

Marks are awarded for:

- Completely unaccompanied horn
- Canon
- Layer-by-layer textural build up
- Riff and sax melody
- Whole orchestra playing in chords.

In a number of cases, the points made were irrelevant or else not sufficiently detailed (e.g. 'alternating time signatures') to gain a mark. This work would be awarded 7/13 ('competent').

Exercise

Draw up revision notes on other aspects of *On the Waterfront*, e.g. melody, harmony and tonality.

SAMPLE QUESTION (D)

'Flying Theme' (EMA 45) is one of the most memorable sections of Williams' score for *ET*. What aspects of the melody and structure contribute to the music's staying power? (13)

Before studying the mark scheme (indicative content) which follows, attempt the question yourself. Notice that the key words are 'memorable', 'melody' and 'structure'. You may find it convenient to refer briefly to the dramatic context of the music, but take care to keep your remarks focused on melody and structure.

Indicative content	
Points should be illustrated with examples from the music.	
Melody	Balanced eight-bar sections
	Two-bar phrases
	Often with same rhythm
	Loosely sequential
	Outlines common chords
	Commanding large intervals and turn
	Mainly diatonic
Structure	Repetitive scheme involving alternation of main and secondary theme
	Variations in orchestration
	And tonality, e.g. appearance of main theme in dominant.

Notice the use of transposing instruments in this score:	
Clarinet in B♭	Sounds a major 2nd below written pitch
Horn in F	Sounds a perfect 5th below written pitch
Trumpet in B♭	Sounds a major 2nd below written pitch

Sample answer 1

	The structure of ET is simple repetition of a principal theme [1], heard for the first time at bars 9–16, immediately repeated at bar 17 [1]. It returns at bars 34–41 in G major, the dominant [1], then again at bars 56–62 in the tonic where it is further varied by imitation in the horn [1], after which there is a coda. ←

Accept: a good point.

	The fact that the theme is repeated so often makes it easier to remember, and the theme itself is also uncomplicated as it is periodically phrased in sets of two bars [1], with rhythmic repetition, e.g. bars 11–12 have the same rhythm as bars 9–10 [1]. The main melody has only a little chromaticism [1], and the big tune has large ← leaps, typically perfect 5ths and octaves [1], resulting in a powerful effect. The strong impression it creates is further enhanced by use of the bright-sounding Lydian scale, shown by the F♯ in bars 75 onwards [1].

Accept for 'mainly diatonic' in the mark scheme.

Examiner's points

There are nine credit-worthy observations, most of them illustrated where possible. The work is systematic and logical and would gain 13/13.

Exercise

Provide examples of any leap of a perfect 5th and larger.

Sample answer 2

• Children's sci-fi film about friendship of 10-year old boy and the extra-terrestrial	All true, but as yet nothing specific has been said about melody or structure.
• Flying theme – written for a 'set-piece' scene with Elliot and ET going for a bike ride in the sky as the sun sets on Halloween	
• Minimalist intro, leading into	Not enough information yet for a mark.
• Main theme in C	
• Repeated throughout the piece [1]	
• Becomes Lydian near the end [1]	Point accepted.
• Structure repetitive	Point already made.
• Some changes in melody and key	More information required.
• Tonal and approachable – different in mood from On the Waterfront	
• Quite dissonant harmony – see sus4 in bar 3 – so a bit more complicated than it first seems	Irrelevant.
• Huge orchestra helps strengthen sound – bells added	Irrelevant.
• Another dissonance is the false relation at bar 74	Not enough precise detail for credit.
• Tension built up by use of pedals	
• Feeling of pedalling given by repetitive rhythms.	True, but irrelevant.
	The final two points are irrelevant.

Examiner's points 🖋

The candidate made two relevant remarks, and would be awarded 2/13 ('inadequate').

Exercise

Write one sentence to establish the context of this music; then list a further six points which the candidate could have made.

Sample answer 3

Mark this answer yourself, commenting at the end on its good points, but also mentioning ways in which it could have been improved. Check your assessment against the examiner's points which follow after completing your marking.

> The music of ET: *Flying Theme* is less to do with
> background effects than creating a single, sustained
> mood to accompany the famous bicycle in the sky
> sequence from Spielberg's sci-fi film. It relies on clear
> melody lines for its effect, and this melody in itself is
> memorable. This aspect of the melody is down to its
> balanced structure of two-bar phrases, and the striking
> shape of the main theme which outlines the common
> chord of C major. It also has prominent intervals of 5ths
> and 8ths which in turn help to give a grand, spacious feel.
> The other point is that you hear the theme
> repeatedly, with some slight changes in minor details, and
> also of key, e.g. the switch to D major at bar 35. There are
> also changes in orchestration, for example, the big theme
> at the start appears in upper strings and woodwinds in
> octaves, while the next time it is doubled by trumpets and
> bells. Bells also appear at the end with glittering effect.
> This bright sound is also partly to do with Williams's
> harmonies. He uses some old-fashioned chords, and
> such effects as the dominant pedal, false relation and
> the Lydian mode (i.e. the F♯) also produces a bright,
> memorable effect.

Examiner's points

Marks are awarded here for two-bar phrases, common chord of C major, 5ths and 8ths, repetition of melody, variation of orchestration in repetition and Lydian mode. The candidate's description of the modulation at bar 35 was incorrect; not all the points were illustrated, and there was a tendency to drift away from the demands of the question. An appropriate mark for this attempt would be 6/13 ('adequate').

Exercise

Provide illustrations for the points made above. Draw up revision notes for other aspects of this score, e.g. harmony, rhythm and texture.

SAMPLE QUESTION (E)

Which aspects of *Tom McElvogue's* (jig) and *New Irish Barndance* (reel) (EMA 61) are typical of Irish folk music? Are there any aspects which are less typical of Irish folk music? (13)

Before studying the mark scheme (indicative content) which follows, attempt the question yourself. Notice that apart from the titles of the two pieces, the key words are 'Irish folk music'. The question is open-ended, and invites you to express an opinion. Remember to address both sides of the question.

Indicative content Points should be illustrated with examples from the music.	
Structure	Double jig with mainly constant quavers
	8-bar sections in jig
	4-bar sections in reel
	AABB scheme for both dances
	Basic material subjected to increasingly elaborate ornamentation
	The breaking-up and re-ordering of components is less folk-like
	Irregular rhythmic subdivisions in reel are less folk-like
Instrumentation	Irish wooden flute
	Foot taps
Modality	F♮s within G major key give Mixolydian effect
	Other chromatic figures point to a less folk-like approach.

Sample answer 1

Tom McElvogue's is a traditional Irish dance. — Not enough information yet.

It is performed on a traditional Irish flute [1], and as often happens in performance, there are accompanying foot taps [1].

In structure, both dances follow the typical layout of repeated strains, alternating to give AABB [1]. Each strain in the jig lasts eight bars [1] and shows modality typical of folk melodies, e.g. the F♮s which are the flattened leading note as in Mixolydian mode [1]. Another typical feature is the ornamentation, especially the treble (three repeated notes), slides and crushed notes [1]. — To be certain of gaining further marks, you need to give locations in the score.

It is obviously folk music, and sounds as though it's performed at a Caily. — Check spelling!

Examiner's points

The candidate made six points, with little illustration. There was no attempt to describe aspects of the pieces which are less typical of folk music. This work would be awarded 6/13 ('adequate').

> ### Exercise
>
> Write a paragraph on the less folk-like aspects of the music.

Sample answer 2

This piece was not performed at a traditional ceilidh but at a recital given in a library, and so cannot be regarded as true folk music.

The performer taps his foot [1], but it proves difficult to create the right atmosphere. The piece only requires a flute – a traditional wooden one [1], but there are none of the traditional elements of Irish music like fiddles and bodhrán.

The first piece is a double jig [1] – with a lot of quaver movement [1], so this is clearly straightforward folk music. It is also made up of balanced eight-bar sections [1] in an AABB pattern [1]. The same structure is used in the second piece, but here the section lengths are only four bars [1] and the increasingly elaborate variation involves rhythmic groups of three quavers [1], e.g. at bar 121, and these are obviously less typical of folk music styles.

This piece shows that even something as rooted in the past as folk music can be subject to development.

Examiner's points

The candidate made eight points, some illustrated, and also tried to answer both sides of the question. The mark awarded would be 9/13 ('competent').

> ### Exercise
>
> The candidate neglected to mention use of ornamentation. List the ornaments employed in the jig and reel, with bar references.

Sample answer 3

Mark this answer yourself, commenting at the end on its good points, but also mentioning ways in which it could have been improved. Check your assessment against the examiner's points which follow after completing your marking.

- This piece provokes arguments about whether it is folk or an artistic attempt at folk music
- Basic traditional instrument – a wooden flute with the performer also tapping his foot
- It is not helpful to talk about folk and art music as if they are separate from one another
- Both the jig and reel have repeated balanced strains in an AABB pattern
- This example of Irish folk music is performed in a concert hall rather a folk club or pub, but still leads to audience participation
- Jig is the double jig type
- Both use ornaments, e.g. trills, mordents etc
- A lot of quaver movement
- The more modern/non-folk aspects include chromaticism
- Though in G, there are strong modal elements, e.g. the F♮ (flattened leading note)
- Other modern features are irregular subdivisions (groups of three quavers) towards the end of the reel.

Examiner's points

The candidate made eight relevant points:

- Wooden flute
- Foot taps
- AABB pattern
- Double jig with quaver movement
- Ornaments
- Modal elements
- Chromaticism
- Irregular subdivisions

There was some illustration, but the work was disorganised. As such, it would be awarded 9/13.

Exercise

Rewrite the above sample answer so that the various points follow on in a more logical manner.

SECTION C: Continuity and Change in Instrumental Music 2011

Set out below are examples of the types of question normally found in this section of the paper. Read them through carefully so that you are sure about the sort of information you are required to provide. If you are uncertain about what is meant, refer to the glossary at the end of this book.

SAMPLE QUESTION (A)

Holborne Pavane 'The image of melancholy' and Galliard 'Ecce quam bonum' (EMA 13)
J. S. Bach Partita No. 4 in D, BWV 828: Sarabande and Gigue (EMA 21)
Four **(EMA 50) as recorded by the Miles Davis Quintet**

Compare and contrast the use of textures in the pieces listed above. (36)

Before studying the mark scheme (indicative content) which follows, attempt the question yourself. Notice that the key word is 'texture'. You may find it convenient to refer briefly to the context of each work, but take care to keep your remarks relevant.

Indicative content Points should be illustrated with examples from the music.	
Holborne	Five-part polyphony
	Equivalent voices
	Generally contrapuntal
	Some imitation
	Imitation by inversion
	Homophony in central section of Galliard
	Bass part less active
	Pedals
Bach	Sarabande contains a variety of textures:
	Chordal
	Monophonic
	Two-part
	With melody accompanied by slower-moving bass
	Free-voiced at cadences
	Gigue is imitative/fugal
	In three parts
Four	Melody-dominated homophony
	Head has melody played by saxophone and trumpet in octaves
	Piano plays chords
	Double bass has walking bass line.

Sample answer 1

A span of three and a half centuries separates the composition of these works, so it is not surprising to find considerable differences in approach to the use of textures. These differences are further magnified by the selection of forces for each work.

Holborne's work is a characteristic example of Renaissance polyphony. Written for five [1] equal parts [1], it is mainly contrapuntal [1]. It involves some imitation [1], but these imitative points are far from easy to hear as Holborne often conceals entries by avoidance of preceding rests [1] or else by using inversions, e.g. bar 1 of Galliard in first and fourth lines [1]. Most of the lines are as lively and melodic as the others, though for harmonic reasons, the bass line is slower moving [1], and even includes pedal-points, e.g. bars 34–39 of the Pavane [1]. The one significant departure from this basic texture comes with the second section of the Galliard which is more homophonic [1].

Texture in Bach's keyboard pieces are more varied. For most of the Sarabande, he uses a two-part texture [1]. Periodically there are chordal passages, as in bar 1 [1], which is immediately followed by a single-line passage [1]. The melody covers a wide range of the keyboard, and uses Fortspinnung, a device whereby the melody is spun out by repetition, sequence, and various forms of intervallic variation. All of this makes for a livelier texture than in the Holborne.

Even livelier is the gigue. This is fugal [1], with a number of imitations at the start of each section before moving into a freer style. In fact this is not really a fugue, because it divides into two clear sections, both repeated, to give the traditional binary scheme – a sign of the Baroque era. The other Baroque feature is the tonality, with a modulation to the dominant at the end of the first section, and to other related keys as the movement goes on.

The texture of Four is not so contrapuntal – in fact it is homophonic [1], although the sax imitates the trumpet throughout the head. There are offbeat chords on piano throughout the piece [1], and later a walking bass for double bass [1], although this one hurtles along at breakneck speed. The melody is in the trumpet, and there are some very interesting effects, e.g. slides, ghost notes etc.

These works are typical of their respective eras, but instead of counterpoint, the complexity of Four arises from the fast-moving melody line and dense, chromatic harmonies.

Notice that the candidate uses the term polyphony here simply to refer to the combination of a number of separate melody lines, and uses contrapuntal in connection with their independence.

Good point.

Unfortunately, although true, the point about melodic writing is irrelevant.

Irrelevant.

This observation is also irrelevant.

This is incorrect. Although they have the same melodic line, the two instruments double each other an octave apart.

These effects come under the heading of melodic decoration.

Examiner's points 🖋

The candidate made 16 often well-illustrated points. Unfortunately, there was considerable irrelevance, and the opening point regarding selection of performing forces was not developed in the course of the essay. This work would be regarded as 'confident', but the digressions would result in its receiving a mark of 24/36.

Exercise

List additional relevant points that could have been made.

Sample answer 2

Four is quite different from the other two pieces as it is homophonic throughout with melody in the trumpet [1]. It is doubled in the Head by the saxophone to make the basic theme stick out. It is preceded by a drum intro and has piano chords [1]. These are typical of the be-bop style, as they are highly dissonant, with many substitution chords.	This is not precise enough. The candidate should say that the trumpet is doubled at the octave by the saxophone.
A prominent feature of the work is the improvisation which goes throughout the piece, although it does not affect the texture which is much the same throughout.	True, but irrelevant.
The other two pieces are much more contrapuntal [1+1 for each work]. Bach uses two-part counterpoint throughout, with melodic writing in the top part. The gigue uses imitation [1], which is only to be expected it being a fugue. The second section kicks off with an inversion of the main theme [X], like many other jigs, and Bach goes on to use other devices like stretto [X].	This observation is misleading, as there are various textures in the Sarabande.
	A misleading remark as Bach does not write fugally throughout this movement.
Holborne's works are typically Renaissance dances with the Galliard a sort of triple time version of the Pavane [X]. It was very common for dances to be paired together, as in keyboard pieces by Byrd and Gibbons. These dances are also quite stylish [X], with much less dance elements than musical. In fact they are so complicated it would be very difficult to dance to. Quite apart from that, they sound dead gloomy, and in any case, when performed on viles, you can hardly hear what's going on. The beat is far from clear.	The candidate here means 'stylised', a term which denotes that, in this case, the dance-like aspects of the music, though present, are much weakened.
	An unfortunate confusion of words here!

> With the Holborne, theres a lot of counterpoint, with
> all the players doing their own thing. The writing is not
> particularly idiomatic, as these pieces can be played on any
> instrument. Theres some imitation in these peices [1], e.g. b.
> 34 and 35, top and middle lines. One thing Holborne has in
> common with Four is the chordal writing in the Galliard, which
> all goes to show that nothing much changes down the years.

Point already credited.

This is not precisely located.

Examiner's points

The candidate made six relevant observations, with limited illustration. There were numerous errors, and the quality of written communication was ungainly at times. This work would come into the 'basic' category, and be awarded 15/36.

Exercise
Improve the quality of written communication of this essay.

Sample answer 3

Mark this answer yourself, commenting at the end on its good points, but also mentioning ways in which it could have been improved. Check your assessment against the examiner's points which follow after completing your marking.

> Textures change from one period to another and from
> one work to another, even within the same period. One
> of the factors which influences the use of textures is
> the instruments being used. The Holborne is for five
> instruments and therefore has a thick texture, while
> the Bach is for harpsichord and therefore sounds thin,
> and Four is for a much more varied group of performers
> (drums, sax, trumpet, piano and double bass) and so has
> plenty going on, but not quite as much as Holborne.
>   So starting with the Holborne, it is quite
> contrapuntal most of the time. There are five parts,
> all rather vocal in style, because the music dated from
> the period before instruments had developed their own
> techniques. As it says in the Anthology, these pieces
> can be performed on violins, viols or any musical wind
> instrument. (Note to examiner: I have translated this
> into proper English so you won't misunderstand.) In other
> words, these pieces can be played on any instruments,
> just so long the notes fit. Most of the parts play a

similar role, but it is interesting to see that the bass part has less to do. Maybe he wasn't very good, or more likely it helped the harmony if there was a firm, clear support for what was going on above. The other parts tend to have a very similar style, and because the music is from the Renaissance period, it is contrapuntal. Sometimes he also uses imitations, and sometimes he uses inverted melody lines (see opening of Galliard).

Holborne departs from this approach only in bars 9–16 of the Galliard which is more chordal. This movement is in the minor key and closes with a tierce de Picardie as was customary at the time.

The Bach Sarabande includes a wide range of textures, starting with chords, before going on to a mainly two-part texture with the bass moving more slowly than the melody. In contrast, the gigue starts with a fugal passage with three parts coming in in imitation. Unlike the Holborne which is not idiomatic, this is now clearly intended for a keyboard player, and though it can be switched from harpsichord to piano – raising issues of authenticity – it obviously cannot be played on much else.

Finally, Four: this is now highly idiomatic with each instrument having a clearly defined role in the ensemble. The piano has chords supporting the incredibly fast-moving melody for trumpet, packed tight with technical devices which can only be played on that instrument. The bass provides a fast walking bass. The texture is best described as melody-dominated homophony.

Examiner's points

Credit is awarded for:

- Counterpoint in Holborne
- Five parts
- Slower moving bass part
- Imitation
- Inverted imitation
- Chords at the start of the Bach
- Two-part texture with slower moving bass
- Fugal opening of gigue
- Three parts
- Melody-dominated homophony in *Four*
- Walking bass
- Chords in piano.

The other points were irrelevant. Avoid asides to examiners, however helpful they are meant to be. This work was adequate, with 12 partially illustrated points, and would receive 19/36.

Exercise

Cut out the irrelevant remarks in Sample answer 3, and add six fully illustrated observations to help raise the score.

SAMPLE QUESTION (B)

J. S. Bach Partita No. 4 in D, BWV 828: Sarabande and Gigue (EMA 21)
Haydn Symphony No. 26 in D minor, 'Lamentatione': movement I (EMA 2)
Shostakovich Prelude and Fugue in A, Op. 87 No. 7 (EMA 25)

Compare and contrast the use of melody in the three pieces listed above. (36)

Before studying the mark scheme (indicative content) which follows, attempt the question yourself. Notice that the key word is 'melody'. You may find it convenient to refer briefly to the context of each work, but take care to keep your remarks relevant.

Indicative content	
Points should be illustrated with examples from the music.	
Bach	Motivic
	With use of *Fortspinnung*
	Some large leaps
	And broken chord patterns
	Chromatic inflections
	Frequent passing notes and appoggiaturas
	Ornamentation
Haydn	Periodic/balanced phrasing in first subject
	Irregular phrasing in second subject because of
	Plainsong influence
	Modal inflections in second subject
	Appoggiaturas
	Repeated note pattern in parts of second subject
Shostakovich	Motivic ('turn' figure and leaping motif)
	Fugue built on broken-chord figures
	Prelude is more chromatic, especially in central section.

Remember that in the Haydn Symphony, the horn in D is transposed down a minor 7th.

Sample answer 1

Melodic writing in the Bach and Shostakovich keyboard works is similar in general approach, while the Haydn is obviously in Classical style. The similarity between Bach and Shostakovich is not as surprising as it may seem at first, as Shostakovich wrote his cycle of 24 Preludes and Fugues as a tribute to Bach on the bicentenary of his death.

> A good opening paragraph, establishing some useful context and setting out a possible line of argument.

Bach's writing in the Sarabande in particular is highly motivic [1]. After the first two bars – the chordal opening and monophonic line which follows – he settles into a melody and accompaniment section. The melody demonstrates the workings of *Fortspinnung* [1], with a gradual unfolding of the melody with the basic material constantly elaborated. The way the very first three notes are treated provides many good examples. The opening stepwise descent is inverted in bar 5 [1] and then heard a fifth higher in bar 6 [1]. The rhythm of two demisemiquavers, quaver and semiquaver, is modified in bar 7 to end with two demisemiquavers [1].

There are also other typical Baroque traits, such as the ornamentation, e.g. the mordent in bar 1 [1], but it is the motivic approach which Shostakovich picked up from Bach [1]. The Prelude opens with a sort of inverted turn (AGAB) which then leads to the leaping figure which sounds much more 20th-century [1]. These ideas are subject to development throughout the Prelude, e.g. in bar 4 Shostakovich switches the order of the last two groups of quavers [1], and in bar 5, the original four-note semiquaver figure is extended to six notes and the 'turn' pattern inverted [1].

In contrast, Haydn uses clearly balanced phrases for much of the time, although the second subject contains irregular phrase-lengths, chiefly because this part of the movement was derived from plainsong sources and Haydn had to adapt free rhythm music to fit in with a fixed time signature [1]. He uses typical Classical devices such as appoggiaturas [1], and occasional chromatic alterations [1].

> Not precise enough.

Examiner's points

The candidate made 12 points, some of which were illustrated. Writing skills showed competence, although the essay would have benefited from a conclusion. This work would be awarded 20/36.

> ## Exercise
> List additional points you would expect to see in this essay, and write a concluding paragraph.

Sample answer 2

All the works have melodies. In Bach it appears mainly in the right-hand parts, except in the gigue where it sometimes comes in the left hand. In the Haydn, it can be seen in the first violin and oboe most of the time, though it can pop up in other lines as well. In the Shostakovich, it is sometimes in the right hand and sometimes in the left. Bach has a motivic approach [1]. In fact most music has motives, otherwise it would not have a reason for doing what it does. Shostakovich uses common chords for his fugue subject [1]. The result of this is that there is no dissonance at all. This is very unusual for Shostakovich, and for music in general. In fact the Bach is packed with all sorts of discord, and even Haydn uses them, e.g. bar 117 where you hear a B, C and a D altogether. Discords mainly arise from suspensions, and there are plenty of these in the Bach, but not so many in Haydn who chiefly uses appoggiaturas [1].

All the composers use chromaticisms. In the Shostakovich they come mainly in the middle part of the Prelude [1] which leads him into all sorts of remote tonal regions. Its still quite easy to play, even though it is mainly on the black notes here (C♯ etc). There is also sharps and flats in the Haydn, but as string players don't have black notes to worry about, it is all a good bit simpler. The Haydn is a classical piece, and there are balanced phrases at the beginning [1]. In contrast, the Bach and Shostakovich just keep going on and on for as long as it takes.

Not the most elegant way of expressing this (irrelevant) idea.

When answering melody questions, the focus must be on the melody itself, not the way in which it is performed.

The point about dissonance here is irrelevant, and the example given is a misreading of the score as the candidate has not allowed for the horn's transposition.

Incorrect spelling: apostrophe required.

Too vague for a mark.

Not enough information for credit.

Examiner's points

The candidate made five points. Much of the writing was irrelevant, confused and illogical. It would be awarded 11/36.

> ### Exercise
> Cut out the irrelevant remarks, and expand on the remaining statements.

Sample answer 3

Mark this answer yourself, commenting at the end on its good points, but also mentioning ways in which it could have been improved. Check your assessment against the examiner's points which follow after completing your marking.

Bach	Haydn	Shostakovich
• D major • Some ornaments • Chromatic at times • Suspensions • Passing notes • Auxiliary notes • Fortspinnung • Contrapuntal in gigue • Sort of fugue • Uses arpeggios	• D minor • Question-and-Answer phrasing • Appoggiaturas • Pedals	• A major • Two motifs: • Four-note figure and wide leaps figure often modified with melody in LH as well as RH • Common chord figure in fugue

There are lots of things which these pieces have in common, like motives, but the Haydn is the only one to have antecedent and consequent phrasing. The other two are not balanced.

Examiner's points

Credit could be given under Bach for ornaments, passing notes, auxiliary notes and *Fortspinnung*; under Haydn for appoggiaturas (not 'question and answer' as the student did not specify the first subject); and under Shostakovich, the use of two motives and the description of them. There were then seven unillustrated points, which would normally earn a mark of approximately 15/36 at the most. This work, however, is not written in continuous prose, and so a lower mark would have to be given, i.e. 9/36.

Exercise

Rewrite Sample answer 3 in continuous prose, providing illustrations for those points which are correct and relevant.

SAMPLE QUESTION (C)

Haydn Symphony No 26 in D minor, 'Lamentatione': movement I (EMA 2)
Brahms Piano Quintet in F minor, Op. 34: movement III (EMA 18)
Duke Ellington and his Orchestra – *Black and Tan Fantasy* (EMA 49)

Compare and contrast the use of harmony and tonality in the three pieces listed above. (36)

Before studying the mark scheme (indicative content) which follows, attempt the question yourself. Notice that the key words are 'harmony' and 'tonality'. You may find it convenient to refer briefly to the context of each work, but take care to keep your remarks relevant.

Indicative content
Points should be illustrated with examples from the music.

Haydn	**Harmony**	Functional progressions
		Cadences (perfect and imperfect)
		Circle of 5ths
		Diminished 7th
		Pedal points
	Tonality	Modulations to relative and tonic majors
		Wider-ranging tonal scheme in development
Brahms	**Harmony**	Functional progressions
		Secondary dominants
		Pedal points
		Chromatic chords, e.g. augmented 6ths
		Occasional open-5th chords
	Tonality	Minor, with some modality
		Wide-ranging key scheme
Ellington	**Harmony**	Based on 12-bar blues
		Substitution chords
		Circle of 5ths
		Plagal cadence at close
	Tonality	Opens and closes in B♭ minor
		Central passage in B♭ major.

Sample answer 1

Haydn was Classical, Brahms Romantic and Duke Ellington early 20th-century jazz. As about 170 years separates the earliest and latest works, it is only to be expected that there are certain differences between their approaches to harmony and tonality. Partly this is because of developments in forms and instrumentation. Haydn uses Sonata form for the first movement of the symphony, with a typical exposition of first and second subjects, a development where the themes are treated in various ways and then a recapitulation where everything comes back again. In contrast, Brahms uses a piano and solo strings instead of a classical orchestra, and the piece itself is a scherzo and trio, a massively expanded version of the minuet and trio, the sort of movement that Haydn would have written. In complete contrast, the Ellington piece is a 12-bar blues specially written to draw attention to problems of racial segregation.

> This over-extended introductory paragraph also introduces a number of irrelevant points. The first two sentences would have been sufficient to establish some sort of background.

When we come to a survey of harmony and tonality, the first thing to notice is the fact that Haydn uses functional harmony [1]. This means that the music is in major/minor keys rather than in modes or being atonal, and the chords help to define the keys through the use of cadences. There are four of these: imperfect, perfect, plagal and interrupted, though Haydn uses only the first two listed, e.g. the perfect cadence, consisting of a dominant to tonic progression, as at bar 16 [1]. The imperfect cadence also consists of two chords. The second is the dominant, but we cannot be sure of the first chord until we hear it, as any workable chord is acceptable here. Haydn uses an imperfect cadence at bars 98–99 [1]. Otherwise his choice of chords is quite limited.

> At last!

> At this level, it will be assumed that you know what the chord progressions making up the cadences are, and there really is no need to specify them.

Brahms uses a much wider selection, but there are times when there is hardly any harmony at all. This happens at the start where there is just a simple bass note accompanying the melody lines – a repeated C. When the chords come in at bar 22, Brahms changes to C major from F minor [X]. He also uses rhythmic augmentation here to produce a grand effect. The harmony here is rich, as all the instruments are playing. In fact there's a fantastic amount of harmony in the piano part as the pianist has to play lots of notes.

> What is the term for this device?

> A frequent misreading of the key at the opening of this move-ment. The quintet overall is in F minor, but this movement of course opens in C minor.

> Irrelevant.

> A nonsensical statement!

	There are more passages without much harmony,	→ This comment has more to do with texture.
	like the fugato, which has just the viola to start with.	
	At other places, it is difficult to work out the chords as	
	Brahms uses quite advanced keys and lots of accidentals.	
	It is the same with Duke Ellington. This piece is a 12-bar	As with the previous remarks on cadences, it is not necessary to spell out in detail the harmonic structure of 12-bar blues. You would only need to comment on irregularities.
	blues [1] which means you have chord I for four bars, chord	
	IV for two bars, chord I for two bars, chord V for two bars	
	and then chord I for two bars. After this, it just keeps	←
	repeating, except that here Ellington introduces a 16-bar	
	section. He also uses substitution chords [1] to vary the	
	basic progression. Another way of getting variety is at	
	bar 13 where the music changes to B♭ major [1]. Another	
	variation comes at the end where there is a quote from	This remark tells us nothing about the harmony or tonality.
	Chopin's Funeral March. ←	
	Approaches to tonality vary considerably, and this is	
	where the instrumentation comes in. Haydn wrote for a	
	small Classical orchestra, with harpsichord, giving a light	
	thin sound, but not much variety in tone quality. Brahms	
	wrote for piano and solo strings, so although there are	
	not so many players, the fact that they were more skilled	
	and could cover a wider range, results in greater variation	
	in tonality. Tonality is most varied in Black & Tan Fantasy,	
	as Ellington has a much wider range of instruments, and	The candidate has confused tonality – keys and modulation – with timbre, i.e. tone quality.
	so with the rhythm and reeds sections he could get much	
	more contrast in tone colour. ←	
	All this shows how harmony and tonality have	
	changed down the years.	

Examiner's points

The candidate made five points. There was extensive irrelevance and confusion, so under these circumstances the final mark would be in the region of 12/36.

Exercise

Write a paragraph contrasting the approaches to tonality in the three works under discussion.

Sample answer 2

Haydn's Symphony No 26 in D minor provides a good
example of the workings of functional harmony and tonality
[1]. Starting in D minor, the first subject of 16 bars is sealed
off with a perfect cadence [1]. Immediately the music shifts
to F major, the relative major [1], for the second subject. The
development modulates through a wide range of keys [1],
notably G minor at bar 55 [1] and A minor in the passage
closing at bar 74 [1]. Other characteristic devices are the
circle of fifths at bars 56–65 [1] and the dominant pedal
starting at bar 65 [1]. One of the most dramatic harmonic
effects comes at bar 69 with the diminished 7th [1]. The
recapitulation at bar 80 is in D minor [1], and the second
subject is heard this time in D major [1].

> No mark awarded for this, as the key is stated in the title.

Brahms's Quintet, written about 100 years later, is
considerably more complex in both harmony and tonality.
Starting in C minor [1], with a tonic pedal [1], the tonality
is notable early on for its modal inflections, e.g. at bar
19 where Brahms avoids using the raised leading note
[1]. At bar 22, there is a sudden shift to C major [1], and
secondary dominants lead to brief references to A minor
and G major [1]. Brahms then turns back towards C minor
by way of an augmented-6th chord in bar 39 [1], but
as the movement proceeds he touches on a much wider
range of keys, e.g. G minor at bar 57 [1], E♭ minor at bar
67 [1], E♭ major at bar 110 [1]. The trio also touches on
some unexpected keys. It opens in C major [1], but soon
modulates to B major at bar 207 [1]. The return of the
main theme at bar 242 is in a sort of destabilised C,
with B♭ in the bass pulling it towards the subdominant [1].
A further striking tonal device comes at the close of the
movement. As expected it closes on C, but because of the
approach to the chord, this feels relatively weak, in fact more
of a dominant preparation for the next movement in F [1].

> Good, perceptive comment.

In contrast, Black and Tan Fantasy, though perhaps
no less complex harmonically than the Brahms, is
certainly less enterprising in terms of tonality. It starts
in B♭ minor [1], the largest part in the middle starting at
bar 13 is in the tonic major [1], and the music returns to
B♭ minor for the final four bars [1].

> Effective linking contrast.

	The harmony is initially dictated by the 12-bar blues
	pattern [1], but as the piece unfolds, Ellington uses some
	unusual additional harmonies, e.g. the Gb^7 at bar 13 which
	working as a German 6th leads onto the tonic Bb major
	at bar 15 [1]. Other noteworthy features include the
	diminished 7th in bar 58 [1], the circle of 5ths at bars
	19–21 [1] and the final string of plagal cadences [1].

The mark is not for reading off the chord indication, but describing its function.

Examiner's points

The candidate made over 30 well illustrated points succinctly. (Compare this sample answer with the first.) The essay would have benefited from an introduction and conclusion, and so an appropriate mark would be 35/36.

Exercise

Provide a brief introduction and conclusion.

Sample answer 3

Mark this answer yourself, commenting at the end on its good points, but also mentioning ways in which it could have been improved. Check your assessment against the examiner's points which follow after completing your marking.

•	Haydn's Symphony is in D minor. Brahms Piano
	Quintet is also in a minor key (C). Ellington's piece is
	also in a minor key (Bb minor). All three pieces also
	have passages in major keys.
•	Ellington uses substitution chords. The harmonies at
	the start are easy to see: Bb minor, Eb minor, Bb minor,
	F, Bb minor, Eb minor, Bb minor, Gb, Bb, Eb^7, Bb, C^7, F^7,
	then nothing happens for the rest of the page.
•	Haydn doesn't use substitution chords, but he does use
	diminished 7ths. Brahms modulates to C major at bar 22.
	Ellington finishes with a plagal cadence. Haydn doesn't use
	plagal cadences, but he finishes with a perfect cadence.
•	Brahms uses remote keys like B major.
•	Ellington uses substitute chords. Unlike Ellington,
	Haydn finishes in D major. Brahms opens with a tonic
	pedal – the repeated Cs in the cello. Ellington's piece is
	a sort of variation piece built on the 12-bar blues.
•	Haydn uses a circle of 5ths at bar 56. So does
	Ellington. Brahms doesn't.
•	Ellington uses pitch bends to vary the harmonies.
	Haydn also uses a dominant pedal.

Examiner's points

Marks can be awarded here for:

* Naming the keys of the Piano Quintet and *Black and Tan Fantasy*
* Use of substitution chords in *Black and Tan Fantasy*
* Diminished 7ths in Haydn
* Modulation to C at bar 22 in the Piano Quintet
* Plagal cadence at the close of *Black and Tan Fantasy*
* Perfect cadence at the end of Haydn's movement
* D major at the close of the Haydn
* Tonic pedal in the Brahms
* 12-bar blues in the Ellington
* Circle of 5ths in the Haydn.

Notice that credit was not awarded for key references which were not located precisely, reading off the chord descriptions from the score of *Black and Tan Fantasy*, and negative statements.

There was no evidence of planning, the whole piece being little more than a random stringing together of facts, not all of which were fully illustrated.

As there were 11 points with limited illustration, but weak organisation, this piece would be awarded 16/36.

Exercise

Organise Sample answer 3, grouping points together logically and providing bar references where appropriate.

Exercise

Using your study guides and any other sources you have, draw up revision notes for all the instrumental works for 2011, making sure you are equipped to write on rhythm, metre, melody, harmony, tonality, structure, texture and general context and circumstances of performance.

Glossary

This glossary is not comprehensive: it refers to terms as used in this volume. For more information about harmonic terms (e.g. suspension), see the *AS Harmony Workbook* and/or the *A2 Harmony Workbook* by Hugh Benham (Rhinegold, 2008). For fuller definitions of other terms and expressions, consult the *Dictionary of Music in Sound* by David Bowman (Rhinegold, 2002).

Alberti bass. A particular type of broken-chord pattern found in classical keyboard music. The notes are heard in the order low–high–middle–high, e.g. in the opening bar of Mozart's Piano Sonata in C, K. 545, it is C–G–E–G.

Anacrusis. Note or notes preceding the first beat of a piece or phrase; this is also sometimes called an 'upbeat'.

Angular. When applied to melody, the presence of wide leaps.

Anticipation. A melody note (frequently the tonic of the key in the highest part) sounded slightly before the chord to which it belongs, thereby creating a dissonance with the previous chord.

Antiphony. Performance by different singers/instrumentalists in alternation. Often – but not always – the different groups perform similar material.

Appoggiatura. A non-chord note that sounds on the beat as a dissonance and then resolves by step (up or down) to the main chord note. The dissonant note is not 'prepared' as a suspension is. Although appoggiaturas are normally approached by leap, accented **passing notes** that are particularly long and/or prominent are often described as appoggiaturas, even though they are approached by step. Some appoggiaturas, especially in the Classical period, were indicated by the symbol ♪, but others are shown as full-size notes.

Aria. A song, usually in opera, oratorio or cantata, for solo voice, with orchestral accompaniment or reduced forces, especially in Baroque music when just **continuo** instruments may be used. An aria often follows a **recitative**, and affords an opportunity for reflection.

Atonal. Atonal music avoids keys or modes; that is, no pitch stands out consistently in the way that the tonic does in tonal music.

Augmentation. The lengthening of the rhythmic values of a previously-heard melody (e.g. where ♪♪♪ has become ♩♩♩). The opposite of **diminution**.

Augmented-6th chord. A chromatic chord which in root position spans the interval of an augmented 6th, e.g. A♭–F♯. The chord also includes the major 3rd above the root (and sometimes also the perfect 5th or augmented 4th).

Binary form. A structure consisting of two sections, the first of which closes in a related key and the second in the tonic. This structure was frequently used by Baroque composers, e.g. in dance movements.

Broken chord. The performing of the notes of a chord one after another instead of simultaneously.

Cadence. A pair of chords signifying the end of a phrase in tonal music. Cadences are of several types, of which perfect and imperfect are by far the most common. *See also* **Imperfect cadence**, **Interrupted cadence**, **Perfect cadence**, **Plagal cadence** *and* **Phrygian cadence**.

Cantata (Italian for 'sung'). From the early 17th century, it could refer to any sung piece, but later came to signify a work for voice(s) and instruments in several movements.

Chorale. A German hymn as sung in Lutheran (Protestant) churches in the time of J.S. Bach. Texts and melodies were often derived from plainsong (i.e. chants associated with Roman Catholic liturgy).

Chordal. A form of homophony in which all the parts move together in the same or very similar rhythm. The term **homorhythmic** (literally 'same rhythm') is sometimes used instead.

Chromatic. A chromatic note is one that does not belong to the scale of the key currently in use. For example, in D major the notes G♯ and C♮ are chromatic. Music that is chromatic contains many chromatic notes.

Circle of 5ths. A harmonic progression in which the roots of the chords fall by intervals of a 5th, e.g. D–G–C–F. The term is also used of progressions in which the roots rise by an interval of a 4th.

Comping. Term associated with jazz and popular music, referring to the playing of a **chordal** accompaniment.

Compound time. A metre in which the main beat is subdivided into three equal portions, as opposed to two equal portions in **simple time**.

Concertino. The group of soloists in a Baroque **concerto grosso**, originally two violins and a cello (as in Corelli's Op. 6 concertos).

Concerto. Most commonly a concerto is a work for one or more soloists (notably a pianist or violinist) with orchestra. In more recent times, it has been applied more generally to orchestral works, implying elements of contrast and brilliance.

Concerto grosso. A concerto in which there are three (or very occasionally more) soloists (*see* **Concertino**) as opposed to one in which there is a single soloist (a solo concerto) or two soloists (a double concerto). Most concerti grossi are from the late Baroque period.

Continuo. Short for 'basso continuo', the continuo instruments form the accompaniment in Baroque music. It may include instruments such as the harpsichord (capable of playing full harmony) and a cello or bassoon reinforcing the bass line.

Contrapuntal. Adjective to describe music that uses **counterpoint**. Counterpoint involves two or more melodic lines (usually rhythmically contrasted), each significant in itself, which are played or sung together at the same time. This is in contrast to **homophony**, in which one part has the melody and the other parts accompany. The term polyphonic is often used as a synonym for contrapuntal (but *see* **Polyphony**).

Counterpoint. *See* **Contrapuntal**.

Diatonic. Using notes that belong to the current key. A diatonic note is one that belongs to the scale of the key currently in use. For example, in D major the notes D, E and F♯ are diatonic.

Diminished 5th. An interval a semitone narrower than a perfect 5th.

Diminished-7th chord. A four-note chord made up of superimposed minor 3rds.

Diminution. The shortening of the rhythmic values of a previously-heard melody (e.g. where ♩♩♩ has become ♩♫). The opposite of **augmentation**.

Dissonance. Strictly speaking, any note not belonging to a triad in root position or first inversion. (Even the 4th above the bass in a second inversion counts as dissonant.) Some dissonances, particularly **suspensions** and **appoggiaturas**, add tension, which in early music had to be 'resolved'; others, notably passing and auxiliary notes, provide rhythmic and melodic decoration.

Dominant 7th. A four-note chord built on the dominant (fifth) note of the scale. It includes the dominant triad plus a minor 7th above the root.

Dorian mode. A scale that uses the following pattern of tones (T) and semitones (s): T–s–T–T–T–s–T. When starting on D, it consists of all the white notes within one octave on a keyboard.

Double jig. Irish dance in $\frac{6}{8}$ time characterised by persistent use of running quavers.

First inversion. *See* **Inversion** (harmonic).

Fortspinnung. The spinning out of a melody line typically by repetition, **sequence**, variation of intervals, **inversion** etc.

Fugal. *See* **Fugue**.

Fugato. A passage in **fugal** style which forms part of a larger of music.

Fugue. A musical form type of piece in which a main theme called a **subject** is treated in **imitation** by all the parts. **Episodes** are the contrasting sections which depart from this pattern.

Functional harmony. A type of harmony that gravitates to the tonic through use of a hierarchy of chords, the dominant being second only to the tonic, and cadences.

Gamelan. An tuned-percussion ensemble from Indonesia (usually from Bali or Java) consisting largely of tuned percussion.

Glissando. Slide from one pitch to another.

Gongan. A rhythmic cycle in **gamelan** music.

Ground bass. The repetition of the same part in the bass while upper parts proceed independently.

Harmonic rhythm. The rate at which harmony changes in a piece.

Head. In jazz and popular music, the basic substance of the number which is then varied. The structure is sometimes referred to as a **head arrangement**.

Hemiola. The articulation of two units of triple time (strong–weak–weak, strong–weak–weak) as three units of duple time (strong–weak, strong–weak, strong–weak).

Homophony. A texture in which one part has a melody and the other parts accompany, in contrast to **contrapuntal** writing, where each part has independent melodic and rhythmic interest.

Homorhythm. *See* **Chordal**.

Imitation. Where a melodic idea in one part is immediately repeated in another part (exactly or inexactly), at the same or a different pitch, while the first part continues. Described with the adjective imitative.

Imperfect cadence. An open-ended **cadence** in which the dominant chord (V) is preceded by any other suitable chord, often I, ii or IV.

Improvisation. Characteristic of jazz, the spontaneous creation of new music, often based on existing musical material (such as a chord pattern).

Interrupted cadence. A **cadence** most frequently consisting of chords V–VI, designed to defeat expectations by avoiding chord I.

Inversion (harmonic). When a chord has a note other than the root in the lowest part, it is an inversion. In a first-inversion chord the 3rd of the chord is in the lowest part, and in a second-inversion chord the 5th. For example, a triad of F major in first inversion is A–C–F, and in second inversion is C–F–A. *See also* **Root position**.

Inversion (melodic). When a melody line is heard upside down, e.g. pitches C–E–D are presented as C–A–B.

Jungle style. A style of jazz developed by Duke Ellington in the 1920s, characterised especially by dark textures and growling brass effects.

Keteg. In **gamelan** music, individual rhythmic cells, the equivalent of bars, which together form the **gongan**.

Lombardic rhythm. A reversed dotted rhythm, with the shorter note first, e.g. semiquaver-dotted quaver. The term 'Scotch snap' is sometimes used to describe this effect.

Lydian mode. A scale that uses the following pattern of tones (T) and semitones (s): T–T–T–s–T–T–s. When starting on F, it consists of all the white notes within one octave on a keyboard. When the fourth is raised in a major scale, this is sometimes termed a Lydian inflection.

Melody-dominated homophony. A melody and accompaniment texture in which the accompaniment is not strictly chordal.

Metre. The metre refers to the pulse of the music and is indicated by the time signature.

Mixolydian mode. A scale that uses the following pattern of tones (T) and semitones (s): T–T–s–T–T–s–T. When starting on G, it consists of all the white notes within one octave on a keyboard.

Modal. A term often used to refer to music based on a mode rather than on major and minor keys.

Modulation. A change of key, or the process of changing key.

Monophony. Music consisting only of a single melodic line. Described with the adjective monophonic.

Monothematic. Music which is based on one theme throughout.

Motif. A short but distinctive musical idea that is developed in various ways in order to create a longer passage of music. The adjective is motivic.

Neapolitan-6th chord. A chromatic chord (often in a minor key) consisting of the **first inversion** of the major chord formed on the flattened supertonic, i.e. the second degree of the scale (in D minor, for example, the Neapolitan 6th has the notes G–B♭–E♭).

Neoclassical. A style which started to become popular in the 1920s. It involved the recreation and adaptation of Baroque and Classical methods and procedures within a more modern idiom.

Nuclear melody. In **gamelan** music, the main theme underlying the various elaborations.

Opera. A large-scale dramatic work for singers and instrumentalists in which the whole text is sung.

Oratorio. A large-scale work on a religious subject for solo voice(s), chorus and instruments in a number of movements. *See also* **Cantata**.

Ostinato. A repeating melodic, harmonic or rhythmic **motif**, heard continuously throughout part or the whole of a piece.

Passing note. A non-harmony note approached and quitted by step in the same direction, often filling in a melodic gap of a 3rd (e.g. A between G and B, where both G and B are harmony notes).

Pedal (note). A sustained or repeated note, usually in a low register, over which changing harmonies occur. A pedal on the fifth note of the scale (a dominant pedal) tends to create a sense of expectation in advance of a **perfect cadence**; a pedal on the keynote (a tonic pedal) can create a feeling of repose.

Pelog. In **gamelan** music, a seven-note scale.

Pentatonic. A scale made up of five notes, most frequently the first, second, third, fifth and sixth degrees of a major scale (for example, C pentatonic is C–D–E–G–A).

Perfect cadence. A **cadence** consisting of the dominant chord (V or V⁷) followed by the tonic (I).

Periodic phrasing. In Classical-period music particularly where phrases of regular length are heard in balanced structures. The expression 'antecedent and consequent' is sometimes applied to these phrases.

Phrygian cadence. A type of imperfect cadence, in which the dominant chord (V) is preceded by the **first inversion** of the subdominant (IVb). It is used chiefly in minor keys, and particularly in Baroque music.

Plagal cadence. A **cadence** consisting of the subdominant chord followed by the tonic (IV–I).

Polychoral. Music for more than one group of performers.

Polyphony. Sometimes used as an alternative term for **counterpoint**, especially in relation to Renaissance music.

Polyrhythm. The use of more than one rhythm at the same time, often implying the presence of different metres.

Recitative. In vocal music, a passage which follows speech rhythms and inflections more directly than e.g. an **aria**.

Reel. In Irish and Scottish music, a rapid dance typically in simple quadruple time.

Riff. In popular music styles, a short repeating phrase.

Ritornello form. A structure used in Baroque music in which an opening instrumental section (called the ritornello) introduces the main musical ideas. This returns, often in shortened versions and in related keys, between passages for one or more soloists. The complete ritornello (or a substantial part of it) returns in the tonic key at the end. The term 'ritornelle', used at the end of 'When I am laid in earth' from Purcell's *Dido and Aeneas*, refers simply to an instrumental passage as opposed to one which is vocal.

Rondo. A form in which the main theme (or subject) returns periodically in the tonic key. Simple rondo takes the form: A–B–A–C–A etc, while sonata rondo involves recapitulation of a second subject as well as the first: A–B(related key)–A–C(development)–A–B(tonic)–A. This form came to be used frequently in finales.

Root position. A chord which has the root in the lowest sounding part.

Scat. In jazz, the singing of 'nonsense' sounds in place of words.

Scherzo. A fast movement which eventually replaced the minuet of the Classical era.

Scotch snap. *See* **Lombardic rhythm**.

Second inversion. *See* **Inversion**.

Secondary dominant. A dominant chord formed on the 5th of any diatonic triad other than the tonic triad itself.

Sequence. Immediate repetition of a melodic or harmonic idea at a different pitch.

Serial. In serial music all (or most) pitches are derived from an underlying fixed series of pitches which can be manipulated by transposition, inversion and retrograding (being played backwards). A widely practised form of serialism in the mid-20th century used a series (or 'row') of 12 notes that included every note of the chromatic scale once.

Sextuplet. A group of six equal notes played in the time normally taken by four notes of the same type. For example, a sextuplet of semiquavers is played in the time taken by four normal semiquavers.

Simple time. A metre in which the main beat is sub-divided into two equal portions. Opposite of **compound time**.

Sonata form. Typical first movement form of the Classical and Romantic periods. In three sections – exposition, development, recapitulation – often based on two groups of melodic material in two contrasting keys (first subject, second subject).

Sprechgesang (German for 'speech-song'). Associated particularly with composers of the Second Viennese School, a form of vocal production in which notes are intentionally not always accurately pitched. Also called Sprechstimme.

Stretto. The overlapping of **imitative** entries more closely than had previously occurred, used especially in connection with **fugal** writing.

Stride. A jazz piano style partly derived from ragtime, in particular from the characteristic left-hand pattern which repeatedly 'strides' from a low note or chord on a strong beat to an often much higher chord on a weak beat. Stride piano was especially popular in the 1920s.

Substitution chord. A chord that is substituted for another chord for the sake of variety. In particular the term is used in jazz.

Suspension. A suspension occurs at a change of chord, when one part hangs on to (or repeats) a note from the old chord, creating a clash, after which the delayed part resolves by step (usually down) to a note of the new chord.

Swung rhythm. In jazz and other popular music, a certain freedom in performance whereby rhythms that might in other contexts be played 'straight' as equal notes are performed with the first of each pair longer than the second, often giving a kind of triplet effect.

Symphony. A work for orchestra with several (usually three or four) movements in different tempi – in effect a sonata for orchestra rather than for one or a few instruments.

Syncopation. The shifting of stress from a strong to a weak beat. For example, in a $\frac{4}{4}$ bar with the rhythm ♩ ♩ ♩, the minim (a relatively long note beginning on a weak beat) is syncopated.

Texture. The relationship between the various simultaneous lines in a passage of music, dependent on such features as the number and function of the parts and the spacing between them.

Through-composed. Applied to music in which the composer avoids repetition of previous material, i.e. fresh material for different phrases in a vocal work.

Tierce de Picardie. A major 3rd in the final tonic chord of a passage in a minor key.

Tonality. Music is described as being tonal when one note is of central importance, other notes being subordinate. The note of central importance is termed the tonic when major and minor keys and scales are used. In 18th- and 19th-century music tonality is established and maintained by **functional harmony**, but tonality can be based instead on other types of scales, notably **modes**.

Triplet. A group of three equal notes played in the time normally taken by two notes of the same type. For example, a triplet of quavers is played in the time taken by two normal quavers.

Twelve-bar blues. A standard chord sequence used in the blues and other popular music, which is based on the tonic (I), subdominant (IV) and dominant (V) chords of a key. Its most common form is I–I–I–I, IV–IV–I–I, V–IV–I–I.

Upbeat. *See* **Anacrusis**.

Walking bass. A bass part that persistently uses the same note length.

Whole-tone scale. A scale in which the interval between every successive note is a whole tone.